Growing Together

A Parent's Guide to Nurturing Child Development Milestones

By
Well-Being Publishing

Copyright 2024 Well-Being Publishing. All rights reserved

No part of this book may be reproduced in any form or by any electronic or mechanical means including information storage and retrieval systems, without permission in writing from the author. The only exception is by a reviewer, who may quote short excerpts in a review.

Although the author and publisher have made every effort to ensure that the information in this book was correct at press time, the author and publisher do not assume and hereby disclaim any liability to any party for any loss, damage, or disruption caused by errors or omissions, whether such errors or omissions result from negligence, accident, or any other cause.

This publication is designed to provide accurate and authoritative information with regard to the subject matter covered. It is sold with the understanding that the publisher is not engaged in rendering professional services. If legal advice or other expert assistance is required, the services of a competent professional should be sought.

The fact that an organization or website is referred to in this work as a citation and/or a potential source of further information does not mean that the author or the publisher endorses the information the organization or website may provide or recommendations it may make.

Please remember that Internet websites listed in this work may have changed or disappeared between when this work was written and when it is read.

Growing Together

A Parent's Guide to Nurturing Child Development Milestones

Table of Contents

Introduction 1

Chapter 1: The Journey Begins: Understanding
Child Development 5
    The Importance of Milestones in Child Development 5
    Physical vs. Psychological Milestones: What's the Difference? 9

Chapter 2: The First Year: Foundations of Growth 13
    Birth to Three Months: Sensory Explorations 13
    Four to Six Months: Movement and Motor Skills 16
    Seven to Nine Months: Cognitive and Social Milestones 20
    Ten to Twelve Months: Communication
    and Emotional Growth 23

Chapter 3: Toddler Triumphs: One to Two Years 27
    Physical Prowess: Walking, Running, Climbing 27
    Language Leap: From Words to Simple Sentences 30
    Social Skills: Play, Sharing, and Empathy 33

Chapter 4: The Preschool Years: Three to Five Years 37
    Fine Motor Milestones and Creative Play 37
    Pre-academic Skills: Colors, Numbers, and Shapes 40
    Emotional Development: Understanding Self and Others 44

Chapter 5: The Early School Years: Six to Eight Years 48
    Academic Achievement: Reading, Writing, and Arithmetic 48
    Social Circles: Friendship Dynamics 51
    The Growth of Independence and Responsibility 55

Chapter 6: The Tween Transition: Nine to Twelve Years 59
   Physical Changes: Preparing for Puberty 59
   Cognitive Complexities: Critical Thinking
   and Problem Solving.. 62
   Social and Emotional Evolution: Self-Concept
   and Peer Relationships 66

Chapter 7: Special Milestones for Diverse Learners 70
   Recognizing Developmental Differences 70
   Navigating Special Education 74

Chapter 8: Health and Nutrition: Fueling Development 78
   Establishing Healthy Eating Habits 78
   Understanding Nutritional Needs at
   Each Development Stage 81

Chapter 9: Technology and Development:
Navigating the Digital Age.. 85
   Screen Time and Your Child's Development................................. 85
   Educating Through Technology: Pros and Cons 89

Chapter 10: Emotional Resilience: Building Coping Skills 94
   Identifying and Expressing Emotions 94
   Strategies for Managing Stress and Anxiety in Children.............. 98

Chapter 11: The Role of Play in Development 102
   Different Types of Play and Their Benefits................................. 102
   Play as a Learning Tool.. 106

Chapter 12: Communicating with Your Child:
A Two-Way Street... 110
   Active Listening and Meaningful Conversations....................... 110
   Fostering Openness and Honesty 113
   Online Review Request for This Book... 116

The Path Forward: Empowering Your Child's Growth 117

Appendix A: Appendix 120
  A: Developmental Milestone Checklist 120
  B: Resources for Parents 124
  C: Frequently Asked Questions about
  Child Development 127

Introduction

Raising a child is arguably one of the most monumental tasks anyone can undertake. From the moment your child is born, you take on the role of protector, teacher, and guide. It's a journey filled with remarkable milestones, countless questions, and occasional doubts. This book is designed to support you through that voyage, offering insights into the physical and psychological development of your child, so you can better navigate each stage with confidence and grace.

Understanding child development is akin to unlocking a treasure chest of knowledge. Each milestone, whether it's a baby's first steps or a toddler's burgeoning language skills, is a clue that helps you understand the intricate process of growth and development. These milestones, while not rigid or uniform, provide a roadmap, highlighting key areas where your child might need additional support or encouragement.

It's important to remember that every child is unique. There's no one-size-fits-all approach to parenting, and what works wonders for one child might not be the best for another. Being adaptable and open to the quirks and individuality of your child is critical. This book aims to equip you not just with facts, but with the wisdom to interpret those facts in the context of your unique child.

In the earliest days, understanding the distinction between physical and psychological milestones can be tremendously beneficial. Physical milestones encompass the observable changes in your child such as crawling, walking, and fine motor skills. Psychological milestones, on the other hand, delve into how your child thinks, feels, and interacts with others. Paying attention to both aspects allows you to support a well-rounded development.

Throughout this book, we will explore each phase of your child's development in depth. Starting from the sensory explorations of infancy to the cognitive complexities of the tween years, you will find detailed chapters that break down these stages into manageable, comprehensible parts. The goal is not to overwhelm you with information but to provide a clear and actionable path forward.

You'll discover how foundational the first year of life is. This period sets the stage for future learning and development. As your baby explores their environment through their senses, develops motor skills, and begins to communicate, you'll gain a deeper appreciation for the subtle and awe-inspiring changes happening daily.

The transition from infancy to toddlerhood marks another exciting chapter. During these years, as children begin to walk, talk, and form social connections, the world around them becomes an expansive playground rich with opportunities. Understanding the importance of play, empathy, and language development during this time is essential for fostering a nurturing and stimulating environment.

As children progress to the preschool years, their thirst for knowledge and social connections grows exponentially. These years are crucial not just for motor and academic skills but for emotional development as well. Teaching emotional intelligence often proves just as important as any academic lesson. Recognition of feelings, both theirs and others', forms a cornerstone of successful interpersonal interactions and long-term psychological health.

The early school years are a time of burgeoning independence and responsibility. Children begin to form more complex social circles and their academic challenges increase. Supporting your child through this transition means more than just helping with homework; it involves encouraging self-reliance and responsibility.

As your child enters the tween years, the changes often feel like a whirlwind. Physical changes signal the onset of puberty, while cognitive and social transformations introduce new complexities. Understanding how to guide them through critical thinking and peer relationships becomes invaluable. This book provides strategies to help you maintain a supportive and communicative relationship during these dynamic years.

Diverse learners present unique challenges and rewards. Recognizing and appreciating these differences ensures every child receives the education they deserve. We'll discuss how to navigate special education and build effective partnerships with educators to meet your child's specific needs.

Health and nutrition are fundamental to your child's development at every stage. Establishing healthy eating habits early on can lay the groundwork for lifelong well-being. Adequate nutrition is linked not only to physical growth but also to mental and emotional resilience. This book dedicates an entire chapter to understanding your child's nutritional needs, equipping you with the knowledge to foster a balanced diet.

In today's digital age, technology plays an influential role in child development. Parents must navigate the fine line between beneficial educational content and excessive screen time. Setting boundaries and encouraging a balance between digital and physical activities is crucial. The goal is to harness the positive aspects of technology without letting it overshadow other critical areas of development.

Building emotional resilience in your child begins early and continues throughout their growth. Children need strategies to manage stress, express their emotions constructively, and develop coping mechanisms. By learning to identify and articulate their feelings, children can build emotional intelligence, which is vital for their well-being and success.

Play is more than just a way to pass the time; it's a powerful tool for learning and development. From imaginative play to cooperative games, different types of play help children develop a range of skills. Encouraging varied forms of play can stimulate creativity, build social skills, and promote physical health. This book delves into these different play styles, showing you how to foster an environment where play is an integral part of learning.

Effective communication is the bedrock of a strong parent-child relationship. Developing active listening skills and encouraging meaningful conversations can foster openness and honesty. Children who feel heard and understood are more likely to share their thoughts and feelings, creating a trusting and enduring bond between you and your child.

This book is more than just a guide; it's a companion in your parenting journey. Each chapter is a step towards empowering you with the knowledge and confidence to support your child's optimal growth. We hope that as you read through these pages, you feel inspired, motivated, and equipped to help your child flourish. After all, at the heart of every great parent is the desire to see their child succeed.

Let's embark on this journey together, armed with empathy, knowledge, and unwavering support.

Chapter 1:
The Journey Begins: Understanding Child Development

Diving into the journey of child development is both exhilarating and profound. Understanding the milestones your child will go through is pivotal for providing the right kind of support and care. These early experiences are the building blocks for your child's future, influencing their physical, emotional, and psychological growth. By recognizing and celebrating each stage, you'll be better equipped to nurture their development, ensuring they build the resilience and skills needed for later life. Let's embark on this path with a clear vision and an open heart, ready to embrace each moment as an opportunity to foster your child's growth and happiness.

The Importance of Milestones in Child Development

Understanding and recognizing milestones in child development is pivotal for every parent. These milestones serve as crucial benchmarks that mark a child's physical, cognitive, and emotional progression. From the first smile to the first steps, each developmental milestone is a triumph in the journey of growth, shedding light on the remarkable abilities your child is developing. Knowing what to expect at various stages helps parents provide the appropriate support, ensuring their child's continued progression and well-being.

Let's start by defining what we mean by "milestones." In the context of child development, milestones are specific behavioral or physical checkpoints that a child typically reaches at certain ages. These checkpoints encompass a range of skills, including those related to movement, communication, cognition, and social interaction. For instance, rolling over, grasping objects, babbling, and recognizing familiar faces are all milestones that occur early in life.

One of the key reasons why milestones are so important is that they provide measurable indicators of a child's development. When your child reaches a milestone, it's a sign that their brain and body are developing as expected. This can be incredibly reassuring for parents, especially those who might be concerned about whether their child is "on track."

That said, it's crucial to remember that each child is unique. While developmental guidelines provide age ranges during which most children achieve certain milestones, they are not strict deadlines. Some children might walk earlier than others, while some may take a bit longer to start talking. Both scenarios can be completely normal. However, consistent delays in reaching milestones might signal the need for further evaluation by a healthcare professional.

Milestones also underline the importance of early intervention. Suppose a parent recognizes that their child is not meeting key developmental markers. In that case, it allows for timely intervention, which is often critical for addressing developmental delays or disorders. Early detection and intervention can lead to better outcomes and can significantly impact a child's long-term development.

Moreover, understanding milestones can quench that ever-burning curiosity about what your child might be able to do next. It turns the process of parenting into an even more engaging experience. Instead of merely overseeing their growth, you become an active participant, knowing what to look out for and, crucially, how to encourage it.

As we talk about these significant milestones, it's essential to distinguish between the different types of milestones: physical and psychological. Physical milestones involve gross and fine motor skills. Gross motor skills encompass larger movements, like crawling or walking, whereas fine motor skills include more detailed actions like picking up small objects using the thumb and forefinger. Psychological milestones, on the other hand, touch on cognitive and emotional development, such as problem-solving skills, or developing empathy for others.

Reaching physical milestones often lays the groundwork for psychological ones. Take walking as an example: once a child starts to walk, they gain a new level of independence which subsequently allows for new social interactions. This newfound ability to explore their environment can lead to better problem-solving skills and social development as they come into contact with new stimuli and peer interactions.

Observing these milestones closely can also influence other areas, such as establishing healthy habits and routines. For instance, recognizing that your toddler is mastering fine motor skills might signal it's a good time to introduce more challenging toys that require precise handling. At the same time, being aware of emotional milestones can help you address your child's needs better, through strategies like assuring a nervous preschooler on their first day or encouraging cooperative play.

In addition to the developmental benefits, recognizing and understanding milestones can reinforce a child's self-esteem. Success breeds success, and achieving milestones gives your child a sense of accomplishment and competence. This positive reinforcement can, in turn, instill confidence and motivation, qualities that are indispensable as they grow older.

Creating a conducive environment for your child to flourish and hit these milestones doesn't necessarily mean providing the latest gadgets or the most expensive classes. It's in the everyday moments—the loving words of encouragement, the times spent reading together, or even the small victories celebrated within the family. These seemingly mundane moments often become the foundation stones for achieving larger milestones.

The concept of milestones also helps parents gauge the efficacy of their parenting strategies. If your child is progressing well, it serves as validation that you're providing the right stimuli and support. On the other hand, if there are delays or hurdles, it provides an opportunity to reassess. It might lead parents to seek additional resources or professional guidance to better support their child's needs.

Understanding the importance of milestones isn't about creating pressure or competition among parents. Instead, it offers a structured approach to observe, understand, and foster a child's development holistically. The goal is not to push your child to meet milestones prematurely but to encourage and support their natural progression.

Milestones provide an experienced roadmap, reflecting collective wisdom from generations, scientific research, and real-world observations. By referring to these benchmarks, you're tapping into a rich repository of knowledge aimed at ensuring your child's growth is both balanced and robust.

In conclusion, milestones in child development should be seen as an empowering guide rather than rigid rules. They help parents navigate the complexities of child-rearing with confidence and knowledge. By understanding and celebrating these milestones, you're contributing positively to your child's physical and psychological growth, ensuring they have the tools they need to succeed at each stage of life.

Physical vs. Psychological Milestones: What's the Difference?

Understanding the difference between physical and psychological milestones is crucial for supporting your child's growth comprehensively. While physical milestones are often more observable and celebrated, psychological milestones hold equal importance. Imagine the delight of seeing your little one take their first steps or say their first words. These moments are markers of physical prowess. But equally significant are the less tangible milestones—when your child first shows empathy or solves a problem independently. Together, these milestones paint a complete picture of your child's development.

Physical milestones, such as crawling, walking, and grasping objects, are about mastering the body and its movements. They're measurable and often happen in predictable stages. For instance, many babies start to crawl between six and nine months. From their first tentative steps to running full-speed into your arms, these milestones lay the foundation for further physical skills. These achievements, though variable in timing from child to child, follow a general sequence and can be anticipated with some accuracy.

Psychological milestones, on the other hand, tend to be more subtle and can vary widely in their manifestation. These involve the development of cognitive, emotional, and social skills. Recognizing these milestones requires a different kind of awareness and sensitivity. For example, smiling socially around six weeks, showing separation anxiety around eight months, or beginning imaginative play around the age of two. These are indicators of healthy psychological development. Observing how a child interacts with others, handles frustration, or responds to new situations provides valuable insights into their inner world.

Both types of milestones influence each other. A child who feels confident and emotionally supported is more likely to take physical risks like climbing or jumping. Conversely, mastering a physical skill can boost a child's self-esteem, enhancing their psychological resilience. When a toddler finally manages to fit that shape into the correct slot, the physical act is accompanied by a surge of confidence and an understanding of cause and effect—a cognitive milestone.

It's essential to remember that each child is unique. There's a broad range of what's considered "typical" for any given milestone. Your child might excel physically but take longer to hit certain psychological milestones, or vice versa. This variability is entirely normal and shouldn't be a source of concern unless accompanied by other warning signs or delays.

Parents often find themselves comparing their child to others, a natural but sometimes counterproductive behavior. It's important to focus more on your child's individual growth trajectory than a comparative timeline. Celebrate each achievement, whether big or small, and offer support by creating environments that encourage both physical and psychological growth. A trip to the playground can enhance physical skills, while reading stories together can boost psychological development by expanding their imagination and understanding of emotions.

When you recognize a physical milestone, it's a perfect opportunity to encourage and stimulate parallel psychological development. For instance, when your child begins to walk, it's not just about the physical act—it's also about independence and confidence. Celebrate their steps not just by setting up obstacle courses, but also by engaging in activities that foster decision-making and problem-solving skills. Let them choose their outfits or decide on the day's snack; these small choices build autonomy and self-esteem.

Conversely, nurturing psychological milestones can provide the context for physical milestones. Teaching empathy and social skills through playdates, for example, not only boosts social intelligence but often encourages physical activity as they engage in cooperative play. Building strong emotional bonds through consistent and loving interactions creates a secure base from which a child feels confident to explore and physically engage with the world around them.

Observing and understanding these simultaneous trajectories allow you to provide more holistic support. Activities that integrate both aspects, such as creative play, can be especially effective. Playing with building blocks isn't just about fine motor skills. It's also a way for your child to practice patience, problem-solving, and even cooperative social interactions if they're playing with peers.

Educational settings also play a vital role. Teachers and caregivers who understand and support both physical and psychological milestones can create balanced learning environments. Incorporating activities that cater to both areas ensures that children develop well-rounded skills. A well-designed preschool program, for instance, includes physical activities like obstacle courses and psychological-enriching activities like storytime and social games.

Parental involvement remains a key factor. Your active participation affirms your child's achievements and provides the emotional support they need to continue progressing. Attentive listening, praising efforts rather than just outcomes, and setting achievable challenges can foster an environment where your child thrives. Engage in conversations that validate their emotional experiences while encouraging physical challenges in a fun and safe manner.

We must also consider the cultural context. Different cultures emphasize various aspects of development, which can influence the milestones' manifestation and perceived importance. In some cultures, early walking might be less emphasized than social milestones like showing respect to elders or communal harmony. Understanding and respecting these cultural dimensions enrich the development process and provide a broader perspective on what it means to grow holistically.

Moreover, watching for milestones helps in early identification of potential developmental delays or issues. If you notice that your child is significantly behind in hitting key physical or psychological milestones, it might be worth discussing with a healthcare provider. Early intervention can be crucial in addressing developmental challenges, ensuring that your child receives the appropriate support to catch up and thrive.

In blending the physical with the psychological, you're building a foundation of overall wellness and competence. Activities like sports can teach teamwork (a psychological milestone) and enhance coordination (a physical milestone). Meanwhile, arts and crafts bolster creativity (psychological) while improving fine motor skills (physical). This nuanced approach not only helps in recognizing your child's strengths but also in addressing areas where they might need a bit more encouragement.

Parenting is a journey filled with surprises, joys, and challenges. By understanding the difference between physical and psychological milestones, you equip yourself with the knowledge to support your child's multifaceted development. It's about fostering an environment where your child feels physically capable and emotionally secure, ready to explore, learn, and engage with the world in a balanced and joyful manner.

Remember, it's not just about the milestones themselves; it's about the exciting journey of getting there.

Chapter 2:
The First Year: Foundations of Growth

The first year of your child's life is a remarkable journey of discovery and rapid transformation. It's a time when foundational growth occurs, setting the stage for future development. From the initial sensory explorations that unfold in the earliest months to the blossoming motor skills, cognitive milestones, and budding social interactions, each moment is a building block. During this critical period, your baby's brain is like a sponge, soaking up every experience and shaping neural pathways that will influence their lifelong learning and behavior. By engaging in activities that stimulate their senses, movement, and social connections, you lay down the groundwork for a thriving mind and body. Remember, the love and encouragement you provide now aren't just comforting—they're essential for nurturing a confident, healthy, and curious individual. This year isn't just about watching your baby grow; it's about actively participating in their journey and witnessing those incredible firsts that form the essence of their tomorrow.

Birth to Three Months: Sensory Explorations

The journey through the first three months of your baby's life is a remarkable period of sensory exploration. Newborns enter the world with a full set of functioning sensory systems—sight, sound, touch, taste, and smell—but these senses are far from fully developed. As a parent, understanding and facilitating your infant's sensory experiences can enhance their development, laying the foundations for future growth.

At birth, your baby's vision is the least developed of all senses. Newborns can only see objects clearly when they are about 8 to 12 inches away from their face. This distance is perfect for gazing into the eyes of those who hold them. High-contrast patterns and colors, especially black and white, are particularly stimulating for their developing visual system. Providing opportunities for your baby to look at books with bold patterns, or simply spending time face-to-face, can help improve their visual tracking abilities.

Parents often notice that their newborns are highly responsive to sounds from their environment. They might startle at loud noises or calm down when hearing a familiar, soothing voice. Infants have a natural preference for the human voice—especially high-pitched tones. Singing lullabies, talking to your baby, and playing soft music can create a rich auditory environment that supports their auditory development.

The sense of touch is critical to a newborn's development. Through touch, your baby learns about their body and their surroundings. Skin-to-skin contact, such as holding your baby against your chest, not only provides warmth and comfort but also supports emotional bonding and security. Gentle massages and soft, textured toys can further enhance their tactile experiences.

Smell and taste are also interconnected senses that play vital roles from the moment your baby is born. Newborns can recognize their mother's scent very early on, which helps create a sense of safety and bonding. Breastfed babies can detect the unique flavor of breast milk, which varies depending on the mother's diet, introducing them to different tastes even before they start eating solid foods. Encouraging these sensory experiences through varied and rich interactions can set a solid foundation for their exploratory efforts later in life.

A newborn's early sensory explorations are not just about passive reception; they actively seek out sensory experiences. You might notice your baby turning their head toward the sound of your voice or grasping your finger when you touch their palm. These actions are early indicators of their curiosity and engagement with the world around them. Encourage this curiosity by offering safe and diverse sensory experiences.

Don't underestimate the simple actions of holding, cuddling, talking to, and playing with your baby. These interactions are essential for their sensory development and also provide opportunities for emotional bonding. The emotional security established in these first few months is a critical foundation for later social and emotional development.

Recognize that each baby is unique and may respond differently to various sensory stimuli. While one baby might love the sensory input of a warm bath, another might initially find it overwhelming. Be attuned to your baby's reactions and adapt the environment to their comfort levels. It's about creating a customized sensory exploration plan that fits your baby's unique cues and responses.

Using a variety of sensory-rich toys and activities can make everyday experiences more stimulating for your infant. Soft rattles, textured balls, and fabric books can provide a tactile and auditory feast that keeps them engaged. Mirror toys, which allow babies to see their own reflections, can also be fascinating for infants, providing visual stimulation and helping them start to understand self-awareness.

As a parent, you play a crucial role in facilitating these sensory explorations. Through intentional, mindful engagement, you can help your baby develop their senses while also building trust and security. This level of engagement sets the stage for lifelong learning and emotional well-being.

Understand that these sensory explorations are not isolated experiences but interconnected processes that contribute to overall development. Enhanced sensory input can lead to greater cognitive and motor skill development, greater communication skills, and more robust emotional health. Encourage a wide range of sensory experiences without forcing them. Your baby will indicate what they find stimulating or soothing.

Encouraging these early sensory explorations doesn't require expensive toys or elaborate setups. Simple activities using everyday household items can provide plenty of sensory input. The crinkle of tissue paper, the gentle swaying of a mobile, or the soothing rhythm of a nursery rhyme can all contribute to their sensory experiences.

In summary, the first three months of your baby's life are filled with sensory explorations that set the stage for future developmental milestones. Each touch, sound, sight, taste, and smell experience contributes to their understanding of the world. Parents can enhance these experiences by providing a rich and varied sensory environment, always paying attention to their baby's cues and comfort levels. Remember, these are the foundational months that pave the way for a lifetime of growth and discovery.

Four to Six Months: Movement and Motor Skills

The four to six month period in your child's life is a whirlwind of physical development and burgeoning motor skills, setting the stage for significant milestones. During these months, you'll witness your little one gaining better control over their head and neck movements, a crucial step towards their burgeoning independence. They'll start to roll over, push up on their arms during tummy time, and maybe even begin to reach and grab for objects, honing their hand-eye coordination. You'll notice their legs kicking with more strength and purpose, laying the foundation for future crawling and walking.

Celebrate each milestone with joy, knowing that these physical advancements are not just about movement but are crucial in building confidence and fostering a curious, exploratory mindset. This phase is immensely rewarding, filled with daily surprises that reflect your child's growth and resilience. Embrace it enthusiastically, as these small steps are monumental leaps in your child's journey of development.

Mastering the Tummy Time signals a critical moment in your baby's journey, especially within the phase of four to six months when movement and motor skills take the center stage. What makes tummy time so pivotal?

Tummy time, in essence, lays the groundwork for many physical and cognitive milestones. It's not just about strengthening the neck, shoulders, arms, and back. It also builds the foundation for more complex movements like crawling, rolling, and eventually walking. It's during these months that your child starts transitioning from passive observing to active exploring.

Initially, many babies might not enjoy tummy time. Don't get discouraged if your little one seems fussy or reluctant. This is completely natural. Start with short, frequent sessions and gradually increase the duration as your baby becomes more accustomed to it. Creating a positive environment is key. Lay down a soft, engaging playmat with colorful toys that can grab their attention and make the experience more pleasant.

Incorporating tummy time into your daily routine can greatly benefit your baby's development. Consider doing it after naps or during diaper changes. The goal is to integrate it seamlessly into everyday activities without it feeling like a chore for either of you.

Aim for a mix of structured and unstructured tummy time. Structured sessions could involve guided exercises, like encouraging your baby to reach for toys or interact with a mirror placed in front of them. Unstructured tummy time lets your baby explore their own movements and develop spatial awareness on their terms. Both are essential.

Moreover, this period is an excellent time to bond with your baby. Get down on the floor with them. Engage with eye contact, talk to them, and gently encourage their efforts. Celebrating their small achievements can make a huge difference. It's these moments that reinforce their sense of security and confidence.

As you've probably noticed, babies grow at an astounding rate. During these crucial months, regular tummy time helps counteract the effects of spending too much time on their back, which can lead to flat spots on the head, known as positional plagiocephaly. Though it might seem minor, this head shape issue can have long-term consequences if left unaddressed.

Let's talk about some practical tips:

- Use props like a rolled-up towel under their chest to give a slight elevation initially.
- Place them on different surfaces, such as a firm mattress, a soft rug, or a yoga mat.
- Spread different textures and toys around to stimulate their senses and encourage turning and reaching.
- Don't be afraid to vary locations, such as moving tummy time from the nursery to the living room or even outdoors on a sunny day.

Watch carefully for signs of fatigue. If your baby seems overly fussy or starts to cry, it's okay to stop and try again later. The goal is quality over quantity. A few minutes of joyful tummy time can be more effective than a longer period filled with tears and frustration.

Another aspect to consider is your posture as a parent during these exercises. Your own body language and enthusiasm can significantly influence your baby. If you lay next to them on your stomach, mirroring their position, it can create a sense of camaraderie and encouragement. You're in this together.

Use tummy time as a photographic moment too. Capture those smiles, curious glances, and tiny reaches. These images won't just be cherished memories; seeing them can also instill a sense of accomplishment in both you and your child. Visual reminders of progress often serve as powerful motivators.

During tummy time, always supervise your child closely. Ensure the environment is safe, free from small objects or hazards. This way, you can confidently allow them to explore and strengthen those muscles without worrying about potential risks.

The broader picture is that mastering tummy time is a gateway to many other developmental milestones. From improved upper body strength, your baby will progress to rolling over, sitting up, and eventually crawling. It's these foundational skills that support later complex motor activities.

Additionally, engaging in tummy time impacts neurological development. This exercise provides visual and sensory stimulation that is crucial for your baby's cognitive growth. The simple act of looking around during tummy time helps develop their visual tracking skills and depth perception, crucial aspects of their overall sensory processing abilities.

Your baby's temperament during these sessions can also provide you with valuable insights. Observing what they like or dislike, and how they respond to various stimuli can help you tailor future activities. It's an ongoing journey of discovery—for both the parent and the child.

Lastly, celebrating these small victories together builds a positive feedback loop. Repeatedly seeing that they're capable of lifting their head higher, looking further, and interacting more actively reinforces their confidence and eagerness to try even more challenging tasks. This period is about fostering a love for movement and exploration that will sustain them through the many milestones to come.

With patience, consistency, and a touch of creativity, you can transform tummy time from a daily obligation into a cherished routine. Ultimately, these formative experiences lay the groundwork for healthy physical and psychological growth, equipping your child with the fundamental tools they need to thrive as they embark on an incredible journey of development.

Seven to Nine Months: Cognitive and Social Milestones

As your baby approaches the seven to nine-month window, you'll notice a remarkable transformation in both their cognitive abilities and social interactions. This period is a time of dynamic change, where your infant is learning about the world in complex and sophisticated ways. The skills they acquire during these months are pivotal building blocks for their future development.

By seven months, many infants start exhibiting signs of understanding object permanence—the idea that objects continue to exist even when they're not visible. This cognitive leap can often be demonstrated through simple games like peekaboo, which suddenly become endlessly entertaining. Your baby's delight in these interactions is not just about having fun; it's a clear indicator of their growing understanding of the world around them.

As your baby continues to develop cognitively, you'll observe them engaging in more exploratory behavior. They might start experimenting with different actions to see the results, like dropping a toy repeatedly. This seemingly repetitive play is actually a crucial part of how they learn cause and effect. Each time they drop the toy and someone picks it up, they're learning that their actions can influence their environment. Encourage these explorations by providing a safe space where they can experiment freely.

Socially, this age range is a period of blossoming personality. You'll likely notice your baby responding more to the people around them. They'll start recognizing familiar faces and react differently to strangers, often displaying signs of stranger anxiety. This behavior can be both charming and challenging, but remember, it's a sign of healthy attachment. It's their way of understanding who makes up their secure base.

At this stage, babies begin to develop stronger attachments, showing clear preferences for certain caregivers. They might cry when separated from you and show joy when reunited. These behaviors are manifestations of a deepening social connection and a more nuanced understanding of relationships. It's important to reassure your baby during these moments, as this helps build a sense of security and trust.

Communication also takes a significant leap. While they might not be forming words yet, their babbling becomes more complex and starts to mimic the rhythm and tones of speech. This is the perfect time to engage in "conversations" with your baby. Mimic their sounds, and then wait for them to respond. This back-and-forth exchange is not only delightful but also critical for their language development. It teaches them the basic structure of dialogue and prepares them for future verbal communication.

Your baby will also begin to understand simple commands and gestures. You might notice that when you say "no," they pause to consider the command, even if they don't always obey it. This burgeoning comprehension is a testament to their growing cognitive abilities. Reinforce their understanding by using consistent and clear commands, paired with appropriate facial expressions and gestures.

Playtime becomes more interactive during this period. Babies start to enjoy social games and activities that involve turn-taking. Simple activities like rolling a ball back and forth can captivate their attention and foster a sense of shared experience. These interactions are vital for teaching them about cooperation and patience, even at this young age.

Additionally, your baby's fine motor skills are developing, allowing them to explore toys and objects in greater detail. They'll start to use their fingers more adeptly, picking up smaller items and manipulating objects with increasing skill. Offer a variety of textures and shapes to explore. Soft toys, teething rings, and safe household items can all become tools for cognitive and social learning.

Amid these milestones, don't forget the importance of emotional communication. Your baby is acutely attuned to your emotional cues. They learn about emotions and how to express them by observing and mimicking your reactions. Show a range of emotions through your facial expressions and tone of voice. This will help them begin to understand and later articulate their own feelings.

You'll also witness the beginning of problem-solving skills during this period. Babies might try to fit objects into different containers or figure out how to retrieve a toy that's just out of reach. These activities demonstrate their growing ability to think logically and strategically. Encourage such behaviors by providing puzzles and interactive toys that challenge their thinking without causing frustration.

Your child's growing independence is another notable milestone. They may start to crawl or even attempt to pull themselves up to a standing position, driven by their curiosity and desire to explore. With this newfound mobility, they'll start to make more choices about where they want to go and what they want to investigate. This independence is essential for their cognitive and social growth, allowing them to see the world from different perspectives.

Finally, it's important to nurture all these burgeoning abilities with plenty of positive reinforcement. Praise their efforts and celebrate their milestones, no matter how small they may seem. Your encouragement builds their confidence and motivates them to continue exploring and learning.

These months are an extraordinary phase when your baby's cognitive and social worlds begin to intertwine more deeply. By providing an environment rich in love, stimulation, and safety, you set the stage for their continued growth and development. Embrace this transformative period, knowing that each giggle, each babble, each milestone is a step towards their future.

Ten to Twelve Months: Communication and Emotional Growth

As your baby approaches their first birthday, their ability to communicate and express emotions takes a significant leap forward. This period, from ten to twelve months, is marked by astounding advancements in how they interact with the world, you, and others around them. Watching your child develop these critical skills not only enriches your bond but also lays a strong foundation for their future emotional and social well-being.

During these months, your baby will likely start to understand basic words and commands even before they can say them. It's common to notice your little one responding to simple instructions like "come here" or "give me the toy." This is because they are beginning to grasp the meaning behind words, which is a giant leap in cognitive development. They are not just learning to talk; they are learning to comprehend.

Emotionally, babies at this stage start to express a wider range of feelings by using facial expressions, sounds, and body language. You'll see them laugh at something amusing or turn away when they're unhappy or scared. This emotional repertoire is fundamental as they start navigating social interactions. One minute they may be beaming with joy, and the next, they could burst into tears if they feel discomfort or frustration. These spontaneous emotional shifts are part of their natural development.

Babies also become experts in non-verbal communication during these months. They might point to objects they want or need or wave goodbye. These gestures are powerful tools they use to bridge the gap between their limited vocabulary and a world full of curiosity and desires. Taking the time to understand and respond to these non-verbal cues encourages them to continue trying to communicate.

Just as crucial to their development is the concept of attachment and bonding, which takes on more depth during this period. Secure attachment with caregivers provides your child a safe emotional base from which they can explore their environment. Consistent and loving interactions reassure them that they are cared for, making them feel safe enough to venture out and interact more openly.

It's important to recognize that this is also a time when separation anxiety can peak. As they become more aware of their surroundings and the people in them, the realization that you aren't always there can trigger anxiety. While this can be challenging, it's a natural part of developing independence. Offering assurance and comfort, while also letting them spend short periods with trusted caregivers can help ease the transitions.

At this age, social referencing becomes a charming and practical behavior. Babies start to look at a caregiver's reactions before responding to unfamiliar situations. This takes the form of seeking approval or comfort and helps them understand how to react based on emotional cues from trusted adults. It's fascinating to see your child glance at you before making a decision, essentially asking, "Is this okay?"

As they edge closer to their first word, babbling becomes more sophisticated, sounding almost like conversational attempts. Enthusiastic "conversations" with your little one, even though their words might not make sense yet, are imperative. Encourage their attempts by responding with genuine interest, which teaches them the back-and-forth nature of communication.

Engaging in activities that stimulate both communication and emotional growth can be immensely beneficial. Reading books together, singing songs, and even simple games like peek-a-boo contribute to developing a deeper understanding and use of language. Each activity you enjoy together builds layers of communication skills and enriches emotional bonds.

Remember, every child develops at their own pace. While one baby might start speaking earlier, another might excel in using non-verbal cues. Observing, understanding, and nurturing your child's individual growth pattern is what counts. Compare less, celebrate more—every small step is a significant milestone on their unique journey.

Encouraging social interaction with other babies and small children during this phase can also help. While your child is just beginning to understand the idea of friendships, exposing them to peer interactions can foster early social skills. They might not be playing *with* other children yet but playing *beside* them allows them to observe and learn.

In the end, your involvement is the key to fostering their communication and emotional development. Amidst the daily hustle, remember to carve out moments of one-on-one time. Your voice, expressions, and touch are vital in helping them navigate this exciting stage. Whether it's through a nightly bedtime story or a shared laugh during playtime, these interactions are golden nuggets in their developmental treasure chest.

As you venture through these final months of their first year, it's essential to keep providing a loving, responsive, and stimulating environment. Encouraging their communication by talking to them frequently and acknowledging their emotional expressions helps build a foundation of trust and understanding. Keep nurturing their curiosity and give them the security they need to flourish.

Your child is growing not just physically but emotionally and communicatively every day. They are building connections, articulating needs, and experiencing an expanding range of emotions. Embracing and supporting these skills during these ten to twelve months will lay the groundwork for their future communicative and emotional intelligence. Celebrate these moments as they mark the burgeoning of your child's unique voice and emotional identity, setting the stage for a lifetime of meaningful interactions and relationships.

Chapter 3:
Toddler Triumphs: One to Two Years

This exhilarating stage from one to two years old is a whirlwind of milestones, where toddlers start to exhibit impressive physical and cognitive abilities. It's incredible to witness as your little one transforms from taking those first tentative steps to darting across the living room and even attempting to climb furniture. Their language skills also begin to flourish, evolving from simple words to forming basic sentences, bridging the gap between their inner world and yours. Socially, this period is marked by budding interactions, sharing, and the early signs of empathy. Each small stride your child makes is a leap toward becoming a more independent and self-assured individual, setting the foundation for lifelong learning and growth. Embrace these triumphs—you're not just watching your toddler grow; you're guiding them through one of the most dynamic phases of their young life.

Physical Prowess: Walking, Running, Climbing

In the journey of toddlerhood, the transformation within the span of one to two years is nothing short of remarkable. During this phase, your child develops key physical abilities that set the foundation for future motor skills. Walking, running, and climbing become not just milestones, but triumphs that mark the boundless energy and curiosity unique to this stage. It's within these actions that we see the burgeoning confidence, the determination, and the joy of discovery that characterizes the toddler years.

If you've been eagerly awaiting those first steps, you're in for a delightful experience. Walking typically begins around the 12 to 15-month mark, although every child is different. Think of this as their first taste of independence. Standing on their own two feet and moving forward unassisted represents a significant leap in development. At first, expect wobbles and tumbles, but that's just part of the learning process. *Patience, encouragement, and a safe environment* are your best allies here.

As your toddler transitions from tentative steps to more confident strides, you'll notice an increase in speed and coordination. By 18 months, many toddlers can walk backward and even start to run, albeit with a certain level of unsteadiness. This is when their gross motor skills are truly coming into play, and the world becomes their playground. Navigating through various terrains and obstacles teaches them about balance, spatial awareness, and physical boundaries.

If you've ever tried to keep up with a toddler running through a park, you know they're driven by an insatiable curiosity. Running not only boosts their cardiovascular health but also enhances their stamina and muscle strength. They may stumble often, but these falls are invaluable learning experiences that teach resilience and the physical limits of their growing bodies. Provide ample space for your toddler to run freely, whether it's a backyard, a park, or a safe indoor play area.

Climbing is another exciting frontier that toddlers eagerly explore. Around 18 to 24 months, toddlers start to climb stairs with assistance and gradually become adept at tackling furniture or playground structures. This phase is driven by a desire to see the world from new heights and perspectives. Climbing challenges their balance, coordination, and problem-solving skills. It's a significant part of their physical development and gives them a sense of accomplishment.

Safety is paramount during this adventurous period. Use gates for stairs, ensure playground equipment is appropriate for their age, and always supervise their explorations. While it's crucial to give them the freedom to explore, creating a safe environment helps prevent injuries. Encouraging soft landings on carpeted areas or using padded mats can protect against the inevitable falls.

It's also a great time to introduce structured activities to support their development. Simple games like "Follow the Leader" can aid in refining their walking, running, and climbing skills. Obstacles courses can be set up using household items to make the experience both fun and educational. These activities provide an excellent opportunity for bonding while also nurturing their physical prowess.

As parents, it's essential to celebrate these physical milestones while understanding that each child progresses at their own pace. Comparisons can often lead to unnecessary worry. Each step, each run, each climb is a personal triumph that deserves recognition and applause. Positive reinforcement helps boost their confidence and eagerness to try new things.

Remember, the goal is not just to hit milestones but to enjoy the journey of getting there. Documenting these moments through photos or journals can help you reflect on their growth and cherish their developmental strides. This stage forms the bedrock of their future physical capabilities, and your involvement plays a critical role in shaping their experiences.

Embrace the chaos, the squeals of joy, and yes, even the occasional scrapes and bumps. They are all part and parcel of growing up. Your toddler's triumphs in walking, running, and climbing are not just markers of physical development but are also emblematic of their growing courage and zest for life.

So, gear up for an exciting, busy phase. Encourage play, ensure safety, and most importantly, be there to cheer them on. These foundational years are fleeting, but the skills they're building will serve them for a lifetime. Celebrate their physical prowess and watch with pride as they navigate the exhilarating world around them, one step, one run, one climb at a time.

In the grand tapestry of child development, these milestones are threads of independence and self-discovery. They may be small steps for your toddler, but they are giant leaps in their growth journey. Embrace each moment, provide unwavering support, and be their biggest cheerleader as they master the art of walking, running, and climbing. Here's to the boundless adventures that lie ahead!

Language Leap: From Words to Simple Sentences

The magical moment of your toddler's first word is nothing short of miraculous. But what's even more awe-inspiring is watching those words transform into simple sentences within the span of a year. This language leap is one of the most exciting developmental milestones during the toddler years.

(maybe 2-4 sentences)

Your child's journey from uttering isolated words to stringing them together is a complex process influenced by both innate ability and environmental factors. By one year of age, most toddlers can say a few simple words like "mama" or "dada." These early words are often accompanied by gestures that help convey meaning. Within just a few months, you'll likely notice an increase in vocabulary, and soon enough, your child will start combining words, forming rudimentary but meaningful sentences like "milk please" or "I want cookie."

Language development at this stage isn't just about speaking; it's about learning to communicate effectively. Repetition, reinforcement, and a rich linguistic environment play crucial roles. Reading to your child, engaging in conversations, and exposing them to varied vocabulary enrich their language skills. You might find it remarkable how quickly they can differentiate between similar-sounding words or grasp the concept of plurals.

Toddlers are natural mimics, and they learn a lot by observing and imitating adults. When you speak slowly and clearly, they pick up new words and sentence structures more efficiently. This is why narrating everyday activities, describing objects, and asking open-ended questions can be so beneficial. For instance, if you're at the grocery store, you could say, "Look at the red apples! Do you want an apple or a banana?"

As they begin to form sentences, toddlers frequently make grammatical errors. These mistakes are a normal part of the learning process. For example, your child might say, "I see cat" instead of "I see a cat." Resist the urge to correct them directly; instead, model the correct usage by repeating it back to them in context. "Yes, you see a cat. The cat is sleeping."

Conversational turn-taking is another valuable skill your toddler begins to develop. By around 18 to 24 months, children start to understand the basic rules of dialogue. Encouraging your child to express themselves and waiting for their response, even if it's a short one, helps build this crucial communicative ability.

Sometimes, a child's pace of language development may seem slower or faster compared to peers. It's important not to panic. Children grow and develop language skills at their own pace. However, if you have persistent concerns, consulting a speech-language pathologist can provide reassurance and guidance. Early intervention can often address any underlying issues effectively.

Creating a stimulating language environment doesn't mean inundating your child with flashcards or incessant drilling of words. Instead, it involves integrating language learning naturally into everyday activities. Singing nursery rhymes, playing word games, and reading storybooks together make the process enjoyable and effective. Toddlers are more likely to show interest and engage when learning feels like play.

At this stage, non-verbal communication still plays a significant role. Gestures, facial expressions, and body language complement verbal communication, helping toddlers convey their messages more clearly. Observing and understanding these non-verbal cues can help you better understand your child's needs and thoughts.

The role of shared experiences in language learning can't be overstated. When you and your child explore new environments together—be it a park, a zoo, or a simple walk around the neighborhood—you're providing fertile ground for language development. Describe what you see, ask questions, and encourage your child to share their observations. These shared moments foster a deeper understanding of the world and enhance vocabulary.

Patience and encouragement go a long way in this journey. Celebrate your child's linguistic achievements, no matter how small. Positive reinforcement, like clapping or expressing excitement, builds their confidence. Avoid showing frustration over mispronunciations or grammatical errors; instead, offer gentle corrections through repetition and example.

As toddlers begin to master simple sentences, they also start to grasp more complex language concepts, like possessives and negation. They'll move from saying "Mommy shoe" to "Mommy's shoe" and from "no want" to "I don't want." These advancements are signs that your child's cognitive and linguistic abilities are flourishing.

Parents might notice an explosion in language skills around the age of two, often referred to as a "vocabulary spurt." This surge can include the addition of new words daily and more complex sentence structures. Your toddler's ability to express their needs, wants, and thoughts more clearly can significantly reduce frustration, both for them and you.

Incorporating language into rituals and routines provides additional opportunities for practice. Mealtime, bath time, and bedtime can be filled with rich vocabulary experiences. For example, discussing the steps of brushing teeth or choosing pajamas fosters both understanding and language use. Consistency in these routines helps cement new words and concepts in your toddler's mind.

While the journey from words to simple sentences is thrilling, it's also just the beginning. This foundational phase sets the stage for more sophisticated language and communication skills. Cherish this time, engage actively, and provide your child with plenty of opportunities to practice and explore language. The seeds you're planting now will blossom into the ability to communicate thoughts, ideas, and emotions with the world.

Social Skills: Play, Sharing, and Empathy

In the journey of parenting, few moments are as rewarding as witnessing your toddler blossom into a little social being. The phase between one to two years is a magical period filled with rapid developments in social skills, an essential aspect of growth that sets the foundation for future relationships. This stage isn't just about physical independence, such as walking or climbing; it's equally about nurturing a sense of connection with others.

Toddlers, in their newfound curiosity, start exploring the world beyond their own needs. The shift from solitary play to a burgeoning interest in others marks a significant milestone. You'll notice your child engaging in parallel play, where they'll play alongside peers without direct interaction. This is completely normal and serves as a stepping stone towards more interactive play.

Play is the toddler's primary method of learning. During this stage, their games become more complex, incorporating imaginative and pretend play. While they may not directly play with others yet, they observe and mimic. For example, you might see your child pretending to feed a toy doll or mimicking household chores. These activities aren't just cute; they're critical in developing an understanding of the world and others' roles within it.

Sharing, however, is a concept that's often challenging at this age. Toddlers are known for their possessiveness—"mine" becomes a frequently used word. This behavior stems from their developing sense of self and the realization that objects can belong to them. As frustrating as it might be for you as a parent, it's a healthy part of development. Gently encouraging sharing without forcing it can instill the value of generosity early on. Using phrases like, "Can we take turns?" or "Let's share with our friend," can make the process smoother.

Empathy, the ability to understand and respond to the emotions of others, begins to sprout around this time. You might notice subtle signs like your toddler comforting a crying peer or showing concern when someone is hurt. These actions, while sporadic, highlight the intrinsic human connection even at a tender age. Reading stories about emotions, playing games that involve caregiving, or simply acknowledging feelings—both yours and theirs—can nurture this budding empathy.

Building social skills isn't just about direct interaction. The environment plays a significant role. Creating opportunities for your child to observe and engage with others is vital. Playdates, visits to the park, or even simple family gatherings become arenas for social learning. The key is variety, exposing them to different scenarios where they can watch, learn, and gradually engage.

Language also ties deeply into social skills. As your toddler's vocabulary grows, so does their ability to express needs, wants, and emotions. Simple phrases like "please" and "thank you" become tools for polite interactions. Additionally, narrating your own actions and emotions helps your child understand and label their feelings. For instance, saying "I'm happy because you shared your toy" connects the act of sharing with a positive emotion.

Encouraging cooperative play is another gateway to building these essential skills. Games that require taking turns, like rolling a ball back and forth or simple board games, help foster patience and social interaction. Through such activities, children learn that cooperation can be fun and rewarding.

Remember, each toddler is unique. Some might naturally gravitate towards social interactions, while others may be more reserved. It's crucial to respect their individual pace. Forcing interaction can sometimes lead to anxiety or reluctance. Instead, offer gentle encouragement and plenty of positive reinforcement when they make social efforts.

Conflict among toddlers is inevitable and a natural part of developing social skills. These tiny disagreements, though often loud and tearful, teach valuable lessons about negotiation and empathy. Your role as a mediator is to guide them through these moments, helping them articulate feelings and find amicable solutions. Rather than simply saying, "Don't fight," try "How about we both have a turn?" or "Can we find a way to play together?"

As your toddler navigates the complexities of social interactions, it's crucial to model the behaviors you want to instill. They learn a lot by watching you. Displaying empathy in your interactions, showing patience, and practicing kind gestures go a long way. Remember, they are little mirrors, reflecting the world they absorb from their closest role models.

Social skills are not learned in isolation; they're interwoven with emotional and cognitive milestones. A toddler who's learning to empathize is also developing cognitive skills by recognizing that others have thoughts and feelings different from their own. These intertwined aspects of growth highlight the importance of a holistic approach to nurturing development.

Balancing praise and guidance is vital. Too much praise for simple social interactions can create dependency on validation, while too little might not reinforce positive behavior. Find a middle ground where your child feels encouraged but not pressured. Celebrate their small victories in sharing and empathy with genuine enthusiasm.

In sum, the social strides your toddler makes between one and two years are the building blocks for lifelong interpersonal skills. These early experiences of play, sharing, and empathy lay the groundwork for future interactions, teaching them the values of kindness, cooperation, and understanding. As parents, your support, patience, and example are invaluable, creating a rich environment where your child's social abilities can flourish.

Chapter 4:
The Preschool Years:
Three to Five Years

The preschool years, spanning ages three through five, are a whirlwind of discovery, growth, and exuberant exploration. This period showcases remarkable strides in your child's development, as fine motor skills enhance through creative play and early academic abilities start to blossom. During these years, kids begin to recognize colors, numbers, and shapes, forming the foundation for future learning. Emotionally, preschoolers become more adept at understanding themselves and others, laying the groundwork for emotional intelligence. These developmental advancements are profound, but what's most inspiring is witnessing your child's unique personality and preferences take shape. Nurture this explosion of growth with a blend of patience, support, and encouragement, knowing that your efforts will foster a confident, curious, and capable young individual.

Fine Motor Milestones and Creative Play

As your child transitions from a toddler to a preschooler, their fine motor skills undergo significant transformations. These advancements are not just about mastering the ability to manipulate small objects but also about cultivating creativity and self-expression. Fine motor skills, the coordinated movements of the small muscles in the hands and fingers, play a crucial role in a child's overall development. These skills contribute to independence in daily activities and serve as foundational abilities for academic readiness.

Between the ages of three and five, children develop increasingly refined hand-eye coordination. You'll start to see more precise movements as they learn to hold and use writing tools, such as crayons and markers. This period is often marked by the ability to draw basic shapes, which gradually merge into more complex forms like people, animals, and other imaginative figures. Every squiggle and doodle is a milestone in itself, representing the blossoming of their artistic capabilities and cognitive growth.

Encouraging creative play is essential during this phase. Simple, everyday items like building blocks, puzzles, and beads can significantly enhance fine motor skills. Activities that involve pinching, threading, or stacking not only improve dexterity but also foster problem-solving abilities. These types of play are rich with opportunities for children to experiment, make mistakes, and learn, which are critical for cognitive development.

Beyond artistic endeavors, fine motor milestones are evident in self-care skills. By the age of four, many children can dress and undress themselves with minimal assistance. They might still struggle with buttons and shoelaces but will gradually improve with practice. This newfound independence is thrilling for them and builds self-confidence. Encouraging your child to participate in activities like setting the table or turning the pages of a book can further refine these skills.

Scissor skills are another hallmark of this age group. Initially, cutting along simple straight lines will be a challenge, but with practice, children will progress to more complex shapes. Introduce safety scissors and supervise activities to ensure a safe and productive learning environment. These exercises are not just about cutting paper; they are about mastering control, concentration, and persistence.

Playdough is a timeless favorite for refining fine motor skills, offering endless possibilities for creation and manipulation. Rolling, flattening, and sculpting playdough strengthens the small muscles in the hands and fingers, preparing them for more intricate tasks like writing. Adding accessories like plastic knives, cookie cutters, or stampers can make this activity even more engaging and beneficial.

Crafting activities provide another excellent opportunity for nurturing fine motor skills. Simple tasks like threading pasta or beads onto a string, tearing paper for collages, or painting with brushes of different sizes can all contribute to hand strength and coordination. Encouraging children to use a variety of materials engages different muscle groups and keeps the activities fresh and exciting.

It's crucial to remember that the development of fine motor skills varies significantly among children. Some may exhibit advanced abilities early on, while others may require more time and practice. Patience and encouragement from parents are key components in fostering these skills. Celebrate the small victories and recognize each child's unique pace of development.

Parallel to refining fine motor skills, creative play stimulates cognitive and emotional growth. Pretend play, drawing from the world around them or their imagination, allows children to experiment with different scenarios and roles. This form of play nurtures creativity, problem-solving, and social understanding, as children often mimic adult behaviors and interactions they observe daily.

Introducing musical instruments, such as small keyboards, tambourines, or maracas, can also enhance fine motor development and creative expression. Experimenting with sounds and rhythms encourages sensory exploration and hand-eye coordination. These musical activities often become a joyful way for children to express their emotions and connect with others.

Digital tools and games designed for preschoolers can offer additional avenues for developing fine motor skills. While screen time should be monitored, interactive apps that require tapping, dragging, or drawing can provide a modern complement to traditional hands-on activities. These digital experiences should be balanced with plenty of real-world play to ensure a well-rounded development.

Parent involvement plays an indispensable role during this stage. Being present and engaged in your child's play routines not only strengthens your bond but also provides guidance and encouragement where needed. Simple shared activities, like baking where they can stir and knead dough, offer rich opportunities for practicing fine motor skills while creating cherished memories.

Remember that every activity and interaction contributes to a child's developing fine motor abilities and creativity. Your encouragement, patience, and active participation are the cornerstones of their progress. Embrace this time of growth and discovery, knowing that the skills they build today will serve them well throughout their lives. The joy and pride they experience with each small achievement are the stepping stones to future successes.

Pre-academic Skills: Colors, Numbers, and Shapes

As your child transitions from toddlerhood to the preschool years, a magical world of discovery and learning unfolds. It's a period when your child's curiosity knows no bounds, and the groundwork for academic success is quietly being laid. This is the stage where pre-academic skills in recognizing colors, counting numbers, and identifying shapes come into play. Let's delve into how you can nurture these foundational skills, setting the stage for a lifetime of learning and curiosity.

Pre-academic skills are the building blocks that prepare children for formal education. Think of them as the roots of a tree, grounding and stabilizing future growth. One of the first skills your child often masters is color recognition. By the age of three, many children can name at least a few colors, but each child progresses at their own pace. Introduce colors naturally throughout the day. For instance, ask your child to pick out the "red" apple at the grocery store or wear their "blue" shirt. These small, consistent practices reinforce their understanding in both fun and practical ways.

Numbers are another essential pre-academic skill. Children typically begin to understand the concept of counting between the ages of two and four. This isn't just about memorizing the number sequence; it's about grasping the idea that numbers represent quantity. Start with simple counting exercises. You can count steps as you climb them together or the number of strawberries on their plate. The goal is to make numbers a part of their daily life, so they not only learn to count but also understand the "why" behind it.

Shapes, too, play a pivotal role in your child's early education, forming the foundation for geometry and spatial understanding. At this stage, children start to recognize and name basic shapes like circles, squares, and triangles. Use everyday objects to teach shapes—point out the "round" clock on the wall or the "rectangular" book on the shelf. Shape-sorting toys and puzzles can also be incredibly beneficial, combining fun with hands-on learning.

Creating a stimulating environment is key to fostering these skills. Children learn best through play, so incorporate educational toys, games, and activities that promote engagement. For instance, building blocks not only help with shape recognition but also improve fine motor skills. Coloring books can solidify color identification while nurturing creativity. Interactive counting games can transform learning numbers into an exciting challenge.

It's also important to read to your child regularly. Books for preschoolers often incorporate colors, numbers, and shapes into their storylines, making learning seamless and enjoyable. Stories about counting animals or adventures through a world of colors captivate their imagination while subtly reinforcing pre-academic skills. This shared activity also strengthens your bond, creating a loving and supportive learning environment.

Consider incorporating multi-sensory learning experiences whenever possible. Activities like painting with different colors of finger paint, stacking toy blocks, and even baking (counting and measuring ingredients) can make learning tangible and memorable. Multi-sensory activities engage multiple parts of the brain, enhancing your child's ability to retain and utilize new information.

Repetition is another critical component of learning at this age. Children thrive on routine and familiarity. Consistently revisiting concepts of colors, numbers, and shapes helps solidify their understanding. But remember, learning should feel like a journey, not a race. Allow your child the freedom to explore at their own pace without pressure.

Social interaction also plays a significant role in your child's learning. Playdates and group activities provide opportunities for children to share their knowledge of colors, numbers, and shapes with peers. Collaborative activities, such as sorting colored balls or building structures with blocks, promote teamwork while reinforcing pre-academic skills. These interactions teach children that learning is a shared, communal experience.

While structured activities are beneficial, don't underestimate the power of unstructured play. Free play allows children to experiment with and apply their knowledge independently. It encourages creativity and problem-solving, as they navigate through play scenarios using their understanding of colors, numbers, and shapes. Whether they're organizing a tea party with different colored cups or building a fort from variously shaped cushions, these moments are crucial for cognitive development.

Your role as a parent or caregiver is to provide support and encouragement throughout this learning journey. Celebrate your child's victories, no matter how small they may seem. Praise their efforts when they correctly identify a color or count to ten. The positive reinforcement builds their confidence and fosters a love for learning.

Remember to be patient. Every child learns at their own pace, and it's essential to tailor your approach to their unique needs and interests. If your child shows a particular interest in cars, for example, use toy cars to teach colors and numbers, counting them or sorting them by color. Aligning learning with their interests makes the experience enjoyable and more effective.

If you notice your child struggling with any of these pre-academic skills, consider talking to your pediatrician or an early childhood educator. They can provide resources and strategies tailored to your child's development. Early intervention can address any concerns and ensure your child is on the right track.

In summary, the preschool years are a time of incredible growth and discovery. By focusing on pre-academic skills such as colors, numbers, and shapes, you're setting a solid foundation for your child's future educational success. Engage them through play, incorporate learning into daily activities, and celebrate their progress. Your involvement and encouragement during these formative years will foster a lifelong love of learning, empowering your child to explore and excel in their educational journey.

Investing time and energy into developing these fundamental skills pays substantial dividends, building the confidence and competence your child needs to thrive academically and beyond. These simple yet profound lessons in colors, numbers, and shapes are the first steps in a long and rewarding educational journey, shaping not just students, but lifelong learners.

Emotional Development: Understanding Self and Others

During the preschool years, emotional development takes center stage, as children begin to grasp their own feelings and those of others. This period is crucial for nurturing empathy and self-awareness. Preschoolers start to identify emotions like happiness, sadness, and anger, not only within themselves but also in their peers. Through play and interaction, they learn valuable social skills, such as sharing and cooperation, which foster healthy relationships. Parents have an extraordinary opportunity to model emotional intelligence, guiding their children through the complexities of expressing and managing feelings. By providing a nurturing and supportive environment, parents can help their preschoolers build a strong emotional foundation that will benefit them for the rest of their lives.

Encouraging Emotional Intelligence is a pivotal part of your child's emotional development during the preschool years. As children between the ages of three and five begin to better understand themselves and others, it's essential to foster a space where emotional intelligence can flourish. Emotional intelligence, the ability to identify, understand, and manage one's own emotions as well as empathize with others, sets the foundation for healthy social relationships and personal growth.

In these formative years, children are like sponges, absorbing not only knowledge but also the emotional cues and behaviors exhibited by those around them. As a parent, your role isn't just about providing love and care; it's about modeling and guiding them towards emotional maturity. When you demonstrate emotional intelligence in your own actions, whether through managing stress or showing empathy, your child is learning from you.

One of the first steps in encouraging emotional intelligence is helping your child to recognize and name their emotions. When your preschooler throws a tantrum out of frustration or bursts into tears due to sadness, it's a teaching moment. Help them to articulate what they're feeling, using simple language like "I see you're upset because your tower fell down."

These conversations play a crucial role in their emotional development. By verbalizing their emotions, children start to internalize that feelings are valid and should be expressed. This practice diminishes instances of acting out as they learn healthier ways to communicate their needs and frustrations. Always remember, validation doesn't mean agreement but acknowledging that their feelings are real and important.

Empathy is another cornerstone of emotional intelligence. At this stage, children are beginning to grasp the concept that other people have feelings too. This understanding can be nurtured through shared experiences and discussions. For instance, reading stories together offers opportunities to ask questions like "How do you think the character feels?" or "What would you do in that situation?" These reflective questions encourage your child to step into another's shoes and see the world from different perspectives.

Another practical approach to fostering empathy is encouraging cooperative play. Activities that require taking turns, sharing, and working towards a common goal help young children understand the importance of considering others' needs and feelings. Games, puzzles, and even simple joint tasks around the house can be powerful tools for this integrated learning.

Moreover, it's vital for your child to learn how to manage their emotions constructively. Teaching self-regulation techniques, such as deep breathing exercises or counting to ten, can be extremely beneficial. These strategies provide children with tangible tools to handle big emotions in more appropriate ways rather than resorting to outbursts or feelings of overwhelming frustration.

It's also about creating an environment where it's safe to express emotions without fear of judgment. Let your home be a haven where feelings can be shared openly and dealt with positively. When children feel secure, they're more likely to explore their emotions openly and develop the resilience needed for future challenges.

Incorporating emotional check-ins can be an excellent practice. Make it a routine to check in at different points during the day, perhaps during meals or before bedtime, to ask how your child is feeling. These check-ins not only promote emotional literacy but also strengthen the parent-child bond through open, honest communication.

Peer interactions also play a significant role in developing emotional intelligence. Arrange playdates or group activities where your child can interact with others. These experiences teach them priceless social skills, including how to read social cues, resolve conflicts, and build friendships. Give them the occasional nudge to navigate these perhaps awkward social waters themselves, stepping in when necessary to guide or clarify but allowing them to try first.

Conflict resolution and problem-solving are essential skills that intertwine with emotional intelligence. Naturally, conflicts will arise in any social setting, offering yet more opportunities for learning. When disputes occur, guide your child through the process of finding a solution. Encourage them to express their feelings and listen to others before deciding on a mutually acceptable resolution. This way, they learn that conflicts don't have to end badly and can instead be opportunities for growth and understanding.

Parents can also make use of role-playing to practice these scenarios. Acting out different situations with your child can give them a safe space to test out their emotional responses and learn from any mistakes in a controlled environment. Dramatize conflicts and resolutions, and let them suggest how to handle things to build their confidence and understanding.

Lastly, it's important to surround your child with positive role models. Besides yourself, teachers, family members, and community figures play influential roles in demonstrating emotional intelligence. Choose environments and relationships that model positive emotional behaviors, and talk to your child about what they observe.

Remember, developing emotional intelligence is a journey that won't happen overnight. Patience, consistency, and empathy from you as a parent will create a powerful ripple effect, nurturing emotionally intelligent, resilient, and compassionate future adults.

Chapter 5:
The Early School Years:
Six to Eight Years

As your child steps into the early school years, a fascinating transformation begins. Between six and eight years old, they embark on a journey that solidifies their academic foundation while expanding their social world. They start to tackle reading, writing, and arithmetic with a newfound curiosity and determination. In the bustling social circles of school, friendships start to blossom and become an essential part of their lives, teaching them invaluable lessons in empathy and conflict resolution. Independence and responsibility take on new meanings as they learn to manage schoolwork, chores, and personal care. This period is crucial for fostering self-reliance, encouraging them to make decisions and solve problems on their own. Celebrating their achievements, no matter how small, builds their confidence and prepares them for future challenges. It's a time of exploration, growth, and immense potential, where your support and guidance play pivotal roles in nurturing their evolving skills and personalities.

Academic Achievement: Reading, Writing, and Arithmetic

As children step into the early school years, roughly between six and eight years old, they encounter an exhilarating phase of academic achievement. These foundational years are pivotal in nurturing a love for learning and setting a solid groundwork for future educational success. In this section, we'll explore how reading, writing, and arithmetic evolve during this age, and how you, as a parent, can support your child's journey into the world of academics.

First, let's delve into reading. At this stage, children often transition from learning to read to reading to learn. This period is about more than just recognizing words or sounding them out. It's about comprehension, making connections, and starting to enjoy the magic of stories. Encourage regular reading habits by incorporating nightly storytimes and providing a diverse range of books that cater to your child's interests. Mixing in different genres—from fairy tales to non-fiction—can stimulate their imagination and intellectual curiosity.

When it comes to reading, every child moves at their own pace. Some might quickly pick up chapter books, while others may need more time to feel comfortable. Patience and encouragement play a crucial role here. The goal isn't only to make them skilled readers but to help them develop an intrinsic motivation for reading. Share your enthusiasm for stories and knowledge, and your child is likely to mirror that excitement.

Reading is closely linked to writing. As children become more adept at reading, their writing skills also begin to flourish. They transition from forming simple letters and words to crafting sentences and, eventually, coherent paragraphs. Writing is a powerful tool for self-expression, creativity, and critical thinking, and these skills can be nurtured with a bit of thoughtful guidance.

Encourage your child to start a journal. This can be a daily diary or a more structured writing prompt exercise. Journals offer a safe space for children to express their thoughts and ideas without the fear of judgment. Additionally, providing fun and engaging writing materials—colored pens, themed notebooks—can make the act of writing more appealing.

Interactive storytelling can also boost writing skills. Start a story and have your child add to it. This exercise not only sharpens their writing but also fosters creativity and imagination. Placing importance on neat handwriting is crucial, but remember, fluency and content take precedence over penmanship, especially in the initial stages.

In parallel with reading and writing, arithmetic forms the third pillar of academic achievement during these formative years. Math at this stage goes beyond simple counting—it becomes an exploration of patterns, problem-solving, and logical thinking. Hands-on activities, like counting objects, sorting items by size or color, and simple addition and subtraction, help kids grasp mathematical concepts in a tangible way.

Numbers are everywhere, and making math relevant to everyday life can significantly enhance a child's learning experience. Simple activities, such as measuring ingredients while cooking, counting change at a store, or planning out time for daily routines, can make math relatable and fun. This practical approach emphasizes the usefulness of arithmetic in real-life scenarios.

Games are another excellent way to build mathematical skills. Board games that involve counting, strategy, and problem-solving help in developing arithmetic prowess. Digital apps and online resources tailored for this age group can also provide interactive and enjoyable ways to practice math, making learning feel more like play.

Positive reinforcement is essential in boosting a child's confidence in all three areas. Celebrate their achievements, no matter how small. Praise efforts over outcomes to reiterate that perseverance and a willingness to learn are valued as much as, if not more than, natural talent. Establishing a growth mindset early on ensures that children view challenges as opportunities to grow rather than insurmountable obstacles.

Parental involvement can't be overstated. Engage with your child's schoolwork without taking over. Attend parent-teacher conferences to understand their progress and areas needing improvement. Collaborate with teachers to create a balanced approach to learning that accommodates both school and home environments.

Reading, writing, and arithmetic aren't just academic subjects; they are the building blocks of lifelong skills. These early years provide the perfect window to instill foundational knowledge, ignite curiosity, and celebrate the joy of learning. Your role, as a parent, is not just to oversee homework but to foster an environment where learning is viewed as an exciting adventure rather than a mundane task.

By acknowledging the importance of these formative academic experiences, nurturing a positive learning environment, and actively participating in your child's educational journey, you lay down a robust framework that supports not only academic success but also a lifelong love for learning. So, dive into this chapter of your child's development with enthusiasm and empathy, knowing that your involvement and encouragement are powerful catalysts in their educational journey.

Social Circles: Friendship Dynamics

Navigating the early school years, particularly between ages six to eight, introduces a wonderful yet intricate aspect of child development: friendship dynamics. During this pivotal stage, children's social circles begin to expand beyond the family unit, often playing a crucial role in their emotional and social development. These early friendships form the building blocks of their social skills, self-esteem, and overall emotional well-being.

Children at this age start to cultivate more structured friendships. These relationships are generally characterized by shared interests, mutual affection, and cooperative play. Unlike the free-form play observed during the toddler and preschool years, interactions now are more organized and rule-bound, frequently involving games that require teamwork and understanding of rules.

It's fascinating how at this stage, children actively seek friendships to explore their world. They start forming "best friends" and identify preferred playmates. This is more than just child's play; it's the groundwork for learning essential social skills such as sharing, empathy, and conflict resolution. Observing your child with their friends can provide great insights into their personality and emotional intelligence.

As parents, it's vital to foster these budding relationships. Encouraging your child to participate in group activities, inviting friends over for playdates, and even gently coaching them on how to handle disagreements can significantly benefit their social development. Remember, these friendships, although seemingly fleeting, can often have a lasting impact on your child's self-perception and social behavior.

You might notice that children at this age begin to practice loyalty and understand the concept of trust. They start recognizing the importance of keeping secrets, supporting friends, and sticking by them through thick and thin. However, it's also a period when they might encounter the first experiences of exclusion and peer pressure. It's crucial to guide them through these moments, teaching them resilience and how to stand up for themselves and others.

In these formative years, friendships can sometimes be a double-edged sword. On one hand, they can provide a strong sense of belonging and acceptance; on the other hand, they can be a source of confusion and conflict. Children learn about social hierarchies and may face challenges such as being left out or teased. How they navigate these experiences can shape their social attitudes and self-esteem.

To help your child navigate the intricacies of friendship, model positive social behavior at home. Show them how to treat others with kindness and respect, how to communicate effectively, and how to handle conflicts gracefully. Your actions can offer a powerful template for them to emulate in their own friendships.

At this stage, schools also play a significant role in shaping social environments. Teachers often facilitate group activities that encourage cooperation and teamwork. Encourage your child to discuss their day and the social interactions they experience. Open lines of communication can help you catch any potential issues early on and provide your child with support and advice.

Balancing guidance and independence is key. While it's important to provide support and advice, it's equally vital to allow your child to navigate their social world independently. This autonomy helps them develop their problem-solving skills, sense of fairness, and ability to build and maintain relationships.

Interestingly, children's friendships during these years transition from being primarily based on convenience—like living nearby or being in the same class—to being more about personal qualities and shared values. They begin to appreciate friends for who they are, not just for what they can do together. This shift marks a significant step towards mature and meaningful relationships.

You may find that children also start forming gender-based friendships during this period. Boys may gravitate towards other boys, and girls towards other girls. This behavior is completely normal and reflects their growing understanding of gender roles. However, some children may still enjoy mixed-gender friendships, and that's perfectly fine too.

Another notable aspect of friendship dynamics at this age is the emergence of group activities and clubs. Being part of a team or group fosters a sense of community and teaches children the importance of collective goals and teamwork. Whether it's a sports team, a scouting group, or an art club, these group settings can significantly enrich your child's social experience.

Friendships also impact academic performance. Positive friendships can lead to better classroom behavior and higher academic achievement, as children are motivated by their peers and often help each other learn. Conversely, negative social experiences can lead to distractions and emotional distress, affecting their focus and performance in school.

Monitoring your child's friendships can be quite revealing. Notice whom they talk about the most, their tone when discussing different individuals, and any changes in behavior. This can provide insights into the health of their social relationships and whether they are thriving or struggling. Offering a listening ear and a supportive environment at home where they can express their feelings freely is vital.

Lastly, emphasize the importance of empathy and kindness. Teaching your child to be a good friend is just as important as helping them find good friends. Acts of kindness, small gestures of goodwill, and sincere apologies can go a long way in building strong and lasting friendships. Encourage them to see things from others' perspectives, to lend a helping hand, and to stand up against injustice and unkind behavior.

The social circles and friendship dynamics formed during the early school years are incredibly influential in shaping your child's social and emotional landscape. By providing the right mix of support, guidance, and independence, you can help your child develop the skills and confidence needed to navigate these essential relationships effectively.

Through these early interactions, children learn not only about others but also about themselves, laying the groundwork for a lifetime of healthy relationships and personal growth.

The Growth of Independence and Responsibility

As children enter the early school years from six to eight years old, they embark on a journey towards greater independence and responsibility, both at home and in their educational environment. This stage is pivotal, as kids start taking on simple duties like completing homework, tidying their rooms, and managing basic self-care tasks. They begin to demonstrate a genuine sense of responsibility, understanding the importance of following through on commitments and experiencing the consequences of their actions. Parents can harness this natural progression by encouraging self-reliance through structured routines and supportive guidance. It's crucial to praise efforts rather than just achievements, fostering a growth mindset that will serve them well throughout life. Embracing these changes with empathy and empowerment will not only boost your child's self-esteem but also lay the foundation for developing critical life skills. Watching your child navigate this exciting phase can be incredibly rewarding, reminding us that effective parenting involves a balance of support and letting go, giving kids the space they need to grow.

Fostering Self-Reliance is a crucial milestone within the framework of "The Growth of Independence and Responsibility." At ages six to eight, kids are beginning to understand the world more intricately. They start making decisions, taking on responsibilities, and developing a stronger sense of self. Now, these developments don't happen overnight, but fostering self-reliance is pivotal in scaffolding their growth during these early school years.

As parents, you might be wondering how exactly to nurture this self-reliance. It starts with simple tasks. Allow your child to choose their outfit for the day or help set the table for dinner. These seemingly small responsibilities lay the groundwork for bigger decisions and tasks in the future. Your child learns not only the value of contributing to the household but also gains confidence in their ability to make choices and complete tasks independently.

Imagine your child proudly making their own bed in the morning or packing their school lunch. These acts build a sense of accomplishment and autonomy, both essential components of self-reliance. While these tasks might seem trivial to adults, they are significant steps for a growing child.

One of the most effective ways to encourage self-reliance is through routines. Establishing a consistent daily routine gives children a sense of security and structure. Knowing what's expected of them and when helps them feel more capable and confident. Consistency is key. Whether it's bedtime rituals or homework schedules, routines provide a framework that supports their growing independence.

However, fostering self-reliance isn't just about chores and routines; it involves emotional and social growth too. Encourage your child to express their feelings and manage conflicts with friends. Support them in solving problems independently, offering guidance but not solutions. This helps them develop critical thinking skills and boosts their emotional intelligence.

For instance, if your child forgets to bring their homework to school, resist the urge to rush it over for them. Instead, use it as a teaching moment to discuss the consequences and strategies for remembering next time. Natural consequences are powerful teachers. They help children understand the real-world impact of their actions without parental intervention.

Another aspect to consider is the importance of setting achievable goals. Help your child set small, attainable objectives and celebrate their achievements. This could be anything from finishing a book to learning a new skill. The confidence gained from fulfilling these goals fuels their drive to take on new challenges. Remember, the goal is to build resilience and self-confidence, not to overwhelm them with unattainable tasks.

In the journey of fostering self-reliance, it's essential to strike a balance between support and independence. Too much intervention can stifle a child's growth, while too little can leave them feeling unsupported. Be a safety net, ready to catch them if they fall, but allow them the freedom to navigate the tightrope on their own.

A critical component of self-reliance is also understanding that mistakes are inevitable. Children must learn that failure is not the end but a stepping stone to success. Encourage your child to view mistakes as opportunities for learning and growth. This perspective helps them develop resilience and a growth mindset, essential traits for lifelong success.

You might be wondering how to handle the inevitable frustrations and setbacks that come with fostering self-reliance. Stay patient and maintain open communication. Listen to your child's concerns and feelings, and provide reassurance and encouragement. Celebrate their successes and guide them through challenges with empathy and understanding.

Interestingly, school environments can significantly bolster the development of self-reliance. Teachers play an essential role in reinforcing these concepts. Encourage your child to take ownership of their academic responsibilities. This includes packing their school bag, completing homework on time, and seeking help when needed. When they take initiative in their educational pursuits, it reinforces the same principles you're nurturing at home.

Socially, your child's interactions with peers provide abundant opportunities for practicing self-reliance. Encourage playdates and group activities where they can negotiate, share, and resolve conflicts without too much adult intervention. These experiences are invaluable in teaching them how to navigate social landscapes independently.

Let's not forget about self-reliance in recreational activities. Whether it's learning to ride a bike, swimming, or engaging in team sports, these experiences build physical and mental confidence. They teach children the value of persistence, practice, and the joy of achieving something through their efforts.

Finally, remember that the journey of fostering self-reliance is a collaborative effort. It involves parents, teachers, and the community working together to create an environment that supports and nurtures a child's growth. Your role is to provide the love, guidance, and resources they need to blossom into independent and responsible individuals.

As you move forward in this developmental stage, be assured that fostering self-reliance isn't about creating a child who doesn't need you. Instead, it's about raising a child who feels confident in their abilities, can make informed decisions, and understands the importance of their role within a larger community. It's about preparing them for the complexities of life with the knowledge that they can navigate challenges and celebrate successes independently.

By supporting their journey towards self-reliance now, you're laying the foundation for a resilient, confident, and capable adult in the future. Embrace this critical phase of their development with an open heart and a nurturing spirit.

Chapter 6:
The Tween Transition:
Nine to Twelve Years

The ages of nine to twelve mark one of the most transformative periods in a child's life, setting the stage for the pivotal teenage years. During this time, children undergo significant physical changes as they prepare for puberty. It's a phase where cognitive abilities flourish, and critical thinking and problem-solving skills become more pronounced. As they explore their newfound independence, tweens start to solidify their self-concept, balancing between the need for peer acceptance and the development of a strong personal identity. Parents play a crucial role in navigating these changes, providing the necessary support to foster resilience and confidence. By understanding the physical and psychological shifts of this stage, you can better guide your child through these formative years, ensuring they're equipped with the tools needed for a successful transition to adolescence.

Physical Changes: Preparing for Puberty

Navigating the tween years—ages nine to twelve—can be both thrilling and daunting. The changes happening in your child's body are significant, setting the stage for the transition into adolescence. Puberty marks the beginning of profound physical maturing, and understanding these changes can help you provide the support your child needs.

At this stage, your child's body starts to undergo a series of transformations driven by hormonal shifts. The onset of puberty varies widely; some children may begin experiencing these changes as early as eight, while others may not start until they are closer to thirteen. This variability can sometimes cause anxiety or confusion, both for the child and the parents, but rest assured it's entirely normal.

One of the most noticeable shifts is the growth spurt. You might wake up one day to realize your child seems a couple of inches taller overnight! This sudden growth in height and body size is one of the hallmarks of puberty. It's not just the bones that are growing; muscles, organs, and nearly every part of the body start developing at accelerated rates. Accompanying this growth is an increased appetite as the body demands more energy to fuel these changes.

Another significant change is the development of secondary sexual characteristics. For girls, this includes the budding of breasts and the start of menstruation. Boys will notice their voices deepening, the growth of facial and body hair, and the enlargement of testicles. Both boys and girls will experience increased oiliness of the skin and hair, which can lead to acne—a common and often frustrating part of puberty. Open conversations about these changes can demystify the process and reduce any associated stigma.

Equally important is the surge in hormones, particularly estrogen and testosterone, which regulate many of these physical transformations. These hormones don't just prompt visible changes; they also trigger internal ones, such as the maturation of the reproductive system. It's crucial for parents to provide accurate, age-appropriate information about these developments. Honest discussions about menstrual cycles for girls and nocturnal emissions for boys can alleviate fears and promote a healthy understanding of their bodies.

The physical changes aren't just confined to the obvious. You might find your child experiencing growing pains, particularly in the legs. These pains are typically harmless but can be uncomfortable. Regular physical activity, balanced nutrition, and adequate rest are essential to support this rapid growth phase. Encourage your child to eat a variety of nutrient-dense foods, ensuring they get sufficient protein, vitamins, and minerals to sustain their developing bodies.

Let's not overlook the emotional fluctuations tied to these physical changes. As hormones ebb and flow, your child might experience mood swings and heightened emotional sensitivity. This isn't just them "being difficult"; it's a natural response to the internal chaos stirred by puberty. Here, empathy and patience go a long way. Remind them that what they're experiencing is universal and temporary. Providing a supportive environment where they can express their feelings openly without judgment is invaluable.

As physical self-awareness increases, so does concern about body image. Your child may start to compare their physical development with that of their peers, which can lead to self-doubt or body dissatisfaction. It's essential to foster a positive body image, emphasizing that everyone develops at their own pace. Promote messages that highlight the importance of health over appearance, and be a role model by practicing self-acceptance and positive self-talk.

A sensitive yet crucial aspect to address is hygiene. With the onset of puberty comes an increase in body odor due to more active sweat glands. Teach your child about the importance of daily hygiene routines, including regular showers, using deodorant, and maintaining clean hair and nails. Make this a normal part of their routine rather than something to be embarrassed about.

It's also a time when children might have more questions about sexuality. It's vital to approach these inquiries with openness and honesty. Correct any misconceptions they might have picked up from peers or media. Ensure that they understand the concepts of consent and respect in relationships, laying a foundation for healthy interactions with others.

In these years, visits to the pediatrician become even more critical. Regular health checkups can monitor growth patterns, ensure vaccinations are up to date, and address any concerns either of you might have. These visits also provide an excellent opportunity for your child to learn about their health from a professional perspective and ask questions they might feel shy bringing up at home.

While these physical changes are paramount, don't lose sight of the psychological support your child needs. The journey through puberty is as much about emotional growth as it is about bodily changes. Encourage open conversations and be proactive in educating them about what to expect. Utilize resources like books, educational videos, or even workshops tailored for children entering puberty. Providing them with tools to understand these changes empowers them to embrace their developing bodies with confidence.

Remember, you play a pivotal role as a guide through this landscape of change. Your patience, understanding, and proactive approach can turn these transformative years into a period of growth and fond memories rather than confusion and anxiety. With your support, your child can navigate the physical changes of puberty with ease and confidence, laying the groundwork for a healthy, well-adjusted adolescence.

Cognitive Complexities: Critical Thinking and Problem Solving

As children transition from early childhood into the tween years, one of the remarkable transformations they undergo involves their cognitive capabilities. This stage, spanning ages nine to twelve, is when your child's thinking processes start to become more sophisticated, setting the groundwork for advanced critical thinking and problem-solving skills. This period represents a profound shift from the concrete, tangible world of early childhood to a more abstract, complex realm of thought.

Imagine your child's brain as a fertile garden where seeds of curiosity are starting to sprout. At this age, children begin to ask not just the "what" questions, but the "why" and "how" questions. They start to relish the challenge of solving problems and developing their own solutions. This curiosity-driven exploration is crucial for cognitive growth. Providing an environment that nurtures these emerging skills is essential for their development.

Tweens are now better equipped to understand more complex cause-and-effect relationships. They can hypothesize outcomes and are motivated to test their ideas, refining their thought processes along the way. Gone are the days when they accepted information at face value. Now, they want to investigate and understand the reasoning behind facts. This shift marks the beginning of their critical thinking evolution.

Critical thinking at this age involves evaluating information from multiple sources, comparing and contrasting different viewpoints, and making informed decisions based on evidence. Encouraging your child to question, doubt, and seek multiple perspectives not only sharpens their intellect but also fosters a lifelong love of learning. It's about cultivating a mindset that is open, inquisitive, and reflective.

Problem-solving skills, on the other hand, enable tweens to approach challenges systematically. This is an age where games and puzzles that require strategy—like chess, coding games, or even complex board games—are not just fun but also developmentally enriching. These activities help kids practice and refine the cognitive processes involved in predicting, planning, and executing solutions.

One of the key milestones in this cognitive transition is the development of metacognition—thinking about thinking. Kids begin to understand their own thought processes and learning styles. They start to reflect on how they learn best, which strategies work for them, and can even begin to self-regulate their learning experiences. This newfound awareness is critical for academic success and emotional resilience.

As parents, your role in fostering these advanced cognitive skills is pivotal. Encourage your child to engage in discussions that require them to present arguments, defend their viewpoints, and consider counterarguments. This could be as simple as debating a favorite book character's decisions or discussing the potential impacts of climate change. Such conversations not only sharpen their reasoning skills but also teach them the value of respectful dialogue and the art of persuasion.

It's also beneficial to introduce real-world problem-solving scenarios. Involve your child in everyday decision-making processes, whether it's planning a family trip or budgeting for a school event. These experiences provide practical applications for their developing skills and help them understand the complexity and importance of effective problem-solving.

While fostering cognitive development, it's crucial to be mindful of the balance between guiding your child and allowing them to explore independently. Over-direction can stifle their capacity for independent thought and problem-solving. Instead, focus on providing the tools and resources they need, then step back and let them take the lead. Think of yourself as a coach rather than a decision-maker in their journey toward cognitive mastery.

Moreover, fostering an environment that supports failure as a learning process is essential. Tweens need to understand that making mistakes and facing setbacks is a natural part of growth. Emphasize effort over perfection and praise their persistence and problem-solving attempts, even when they don't lead to the correct answer. This mindset helps build resilience and a positive attitude towards learning.

The emergence of digital tools and resources has also influenced how tweens develop cognitive and problem-solving skills. Educational apps, online research, and interactive platforms can provide rich opportunities for critical thinking and exploration. However, it's essential to guide your tween in using these resources wisely. Discuss the importance of evaluating the credibility of online sources and the potential pitfalls of information overload.

Parents should also be aware of the potential challenges that come with this enhanced cognitive capability. As tweens start to think more abstractly, they may also experience increased anxiety over complex issues like global events or social dynamics. Open and supportive communication is key. Address their concerns with empathy and provide balanced perspectives that equip them to process their thoughts constructively.

At this stage, teachers and educational systems play a complementary role in nurturing critical thinking and problem-solving skills. Encourage your child's involvement in school activities that promote these skills, such as science fairs, debate clubs, or robotics teams. These experiences offer a structured environment where they can collaborate, innovate, and challenge their cognitive boundaries.

It's also beneficial to introduce your child to different perspectives and cultural viewpoints. Reading books set in different parts of the world, learning about global histories, or even conversing with people from diverse backgrounds can significantly widen their cognitive horizons. Such exposure not only enhances critical thinking but also fosters empathy and a deeper understanding of global interconnectedness.

Finally, remember that each child's cognitive development journey is unique. Some may naturally excel in abstract thinking and problem-solving, while others may need more time and practice. Celebrate their individual progress and offer support tailored to their needs. The goal is not to rush them through these milestones but to foster a rich, supportive environment where their cognitive abilities can flourish at their own pace.

In conclusion, the tween years are a significant period for cognitive development, marked by the blossoming of critical thinking and problem-solving skills. By nurturing these capacities with patience, encouragement, and the right mix of guidance and independence, you can help your child build a strong foundation for future learning and intellectual growth. With your support, they will be well-equipped to tackle the challenges and seize the opportunities that lie ahead, prepared to think deeply, solve problems effectively, and continue their journey of lifelong learning.

Social and Emotional Evolution: Self-Concept and Peer Relationships

As children transition from early school years into the twilight space of the tween years, a remarkable shift in their social and emotional world takes place. This period, spanning from nine to twelve years, is marked by significant strides in self-concept and peer relationships. The transformation isn't abrupt, but it's substantial enough to require your keen observation and understanding.

At this stage, children begin to develop a more nuanced sense of self. They start reflecting on their inner world and how they fit into the larger social fabric. This newfound self-awareness often raises questions about identity, values, and individuality. It's essential for parents to acknowledge and support this exploration, fostering a positive self-concept that can be a foundation for future confidence and self-esteem.

Your child's perception of themselves starts to amalgamate experiences from home, school, and interactions with peers. Positive reinforcement, unconditional acceptance, and open communication become your tools in helping them form a healthy self-concept. Be vigilant of their self-talk—how they describe themselves and their abilities. Encouragement and constructive feedback go a long way in shaping a resilient self-image.

Peer relationships during the tween years also undergo a noticeable transformation. Friends become more significant sources of validation and support. Peer acceptance often rivals, and sometimes surpasses, the importance of parental approval. Navigating friendships can be challenging for tweens as they grapple with peer pressure, the desire for inclusion, and emerging social hierarchies.

Parents play an indispensable role in guiding children through these social complexities. Open conversations about friendships, empathy, and the values of kindness and respect can provide the guidance tweens need to form meaningful and positive relationships. Encouraging your child to express their feelings and thoughts about their friendships can help them navigate emotional ups and downs.

It's natural for peer relationships to fluctuate; best friends can change, and new social circles form. Be mindful not to intervene too quickly in your child's social conflicts unless necessary. Providing a safe space for them to share their experiences can offer insights into their social dynamics and equip them to resolve issues independently. Helping them understand that it's okay when friendships shift will promote adaptability.

Bullying is an unfortunate reality that some tweens may face. It's crucial to discuss this potential issue proactively. Equip your child with strategies to stand up for themselves and others, and emphasize the importance of seeking help from trusted adults. Your active involvement in their digital world is just as important—cyberbullying has become a prevalent concern. Open dialogue about online behavior and establishing trust can mitigate risks.

Family continues to be a bedrock during the tween years, even as peer relationships gain prominence. Your support and consistent presence provide emotional security. Family activities, open discussions, and shared responsibilities can reinforce familial bonds and help your child feel connected. Balancing structure and freedom is key; tweens need both guidance and the space to develop autonomy.

Your engagement with your child's school life also impacts their social and emotional development. Building a strong partnership with teachers and understanding the school's social environment can offer additional support. Be engaged without being overbearing; show interest in their academic and extracurricular activities, but allow them to take the lead in how much they share.

Emotional intelligence takes a significant leap forward during these years. Tweens start to better understand and regulate their emotions. Encourage them to identify and articulate their feelings, and model effective coping strategies for managing stress and anxiety. Mindfulness practices, regular physical activity, and fostering hobbies can all contribute to emotional well-being.

As your child's social world expands, so does their insight into the broader community and societal roles. They might start showing interest in social justice, community service, or even environmental issues. Supporting these interests can empower them to feel a sense of purpose and contribution outside themselves.

In conclusion, the tween years are a profound period of social and emotional evolution. Your role in nurturing a healthy self-concept and facilitating positive peer relationships cannot be overstated. By providing steady support, open communication, and a resilient familial foundation, you set the stage for your child's confident transition into adolescence and beyond. This journey, though filled with challenges, is equally brimming with opportunities for growth and connection.

Chapter 7: Special Milestones for Diverse Learners

Understanding that every child is unique, this chapter focuses on the special milestones encountered by diverse learners and the importance of recognizing and appreciating developmental differences. It's crucial for parents to embrace these differences and adopt a compassionate, informed approach to their child's individual needs. By identifying these unique developmental paths early, parents can work closely with educators and specialists to create supportive environments that foster growth and confidence. Navigating special education can be challenging, but building strong partnerships with educators ensures that the child receives the tailored support essential for thriving. Ultimately, the goal is to equip both parents and children with the tools they need to meet these distinctive milestones with resilience and optimism, paving the way for a brighter future.

Recognizing Developmental Differences

When it comes to nurturing our children, acknowledging that each child is unique in their developmental journey can be both a challenge and a joy. It's essential to recognize that children don't all follow the same path, nor do they reach milestones at the same pace. Understanding these differences isn't just about patience; it's about honoring your child's individual growth and offering the right support at the right time.

Every child moves through stages of development in their own time. This means that while one child might start talking before they're a year old, another might not speak until closer to two years. It's crucial not to compare one child's developmental timeline to another's, as each child is working on their own unique skills and abilities. Whether they're mastering walking, talking, or making friends, knowing that there isn't a "one-size-fits-all" approach to development can help you celebrate your child's unique progress.

A significant component of recognizing developmental differences is understanding where these variations come from. Genetics play a significant role, but so does the environment. Factors such as family dynamics, cultural background, and individual temperament can all influence how and when children reach their milestones. Embracing these differences means acknowledging that diversity is a strength, not a setback.

On a practical level, recognizing developmental differences involves paying close attention to your child's behavior and abilities. Are they expressing emotions differently than their peers? Do they seem to struggle more with certain tasks? Having this keen awareness allows you to spot areas where they might need extra support or where they're excelling. It's about tuning in and responding appropriately, helping them build confidence in their own unique capabilities.

Consider this scenario: While one child may quickly master the skill of tying their shoes, they may struggle with forming friendships. Another child might become the social butterfly of the playground while needing more time to build fine motor skills. By focusing on what your child can do rather than what they can't, you help them build a positive self-concept.

Observations alone may not always provide the full picture. Engaging with professionals, such as pediatricians and child psychologists, can be immensely helpful. They provide insights and tools for understanding and celebrating your child's unique developmental journey. Early intervention, if necessary, can pave the way for smoother transitions across developmental stages.

One of the most empowering things you can do as a parent is to foster a supportive environment. Children thrive when they feel safe and encouraged to explore their abilities. This could mean creating a learning space at home tailored to your child's interests or involving them in activities that align with their strengths. Remember, success isn't measured by comparison but by steady, personal growth.

Connecting with other parents can also bring valuable perspectives. Parenting communities, both online and offline, offer a wealth of insights and shared experiences. You may discover that what you're going through isn't unique, and that can be incredibly comforting. More than that, these communities can provide new ideas for supporting your child's development in innovative ways.

At times, developmental differences might manifest as more complex challenges. For instance, children with learning disabilities or those on the autism spectrum might require specialized support. Understanding these conditions and working closely with educators and therapists can make a profound difference. Navigating special education services, for instance, becomes a partnership effort, ensuring that your child receives the personalized attention they need to thrive.

Imagine a child who struggles with reading but has an extraordinary talent for music. Recognizing and nurturing that musical talent can build their self-esteem and provide a channel for expressing themselves. Celebrating what your child brings to the world—not just academically, but creatively and emotionally—cultivates an environment of acceptance and love.

Another critical aspect of recognizing developmental differences is open communication within the family. Encourage siblings to be supportive and understanding of their brother's or sister's unique needs. Unity and compassion within the household can significantly impact a child's development and self-worth. It's not just about the immediate family, though. Extended family members and friends should also be educated about your child's specific journey, fostering an inclusive and supportive community.

It's also essential to adapt your parenting strategies to suit your child's development. Flexibility is key. You might find that your usual approach to discipline or encouragement needs tweaking as your child grows and their needs evolve. This adaptive mindset helps you stay in tune with your child's changing landscape, ensuring that your support remains relevant and effective.

While differences can sometimes be a source of worry, they also present unique opportunities for growth and learning. Teach your child that their distinctive path is something to be proud of. Highlight their strengths and encourage them to embrace what makes them unique. This positive reinforcement not only boosts their self-esteem but also emboldens them to tackle new challenges with confidence.

As you move forward, remember that recognizing developmental differences isn't just about identifying what makes children different; it's about understanding and celebrating what makes them special. It's about building a foundation of love, respect, and encouragement that will support them throughout their lives. By doing so, you're not only guiding your child through their own unique developmental milestones but also shaping them into resilient, confident individuals who understand the value of their uniqueness.

In conclusion, the journey of recognizing developmental differences is as complex as it is rewarding. It's about being there, every step of the way, to notice, understand, and support the unique milestones your child achieves. Embrace this journey wholeheartedly. Celebrate every small victory, offer support during challenging moments, and create an environment where your child feels valued for who they are. Through this approach, you'll not only foster their development but also nurture a relationship built on mutual respect, love, and admiration.

Navigating Special Education

Understanding the nuances of special education is crucial for parents aiming to support their diverse learners effectively. Navigating the maze of special education services can feel overwhelming, but arming yourself with knowledge and advocating for your child's unique needs can make a significant difference. It's about more than just meeting academic benchmarks; it's about recognizing and celebrating your child's individual strengths and addressing challenges with tailored strategies. Collaborating with educators, seeking out resources, and fostering an inclusive environment at home will empower you to champion your child's journey through their educational landscape. Stay proactive, stay informed, and remember that the goal is to ensure your child's growth and happiness in an environment where they can thrive.

Building Partnerships with Educators is essential for successfully navigating the world of special education for your child. As a parent, creating a strong collaborative relationship with educators can significantly enhance the quality of support and resources available to your child, ensuring their unique needs are met effectively. These partnerships are vital for fostering an environment where your child can thrive academically, socially, and emotionally.

Navigating special education can be challenging, but understanding the value of building strong connections with educators and other professionals involved in your child's care can make a difference. Consider it a team effort where everyone contributes their expertise to support your child's growth. When parents and educators work together, it creates a solid foundation for effectively addressing the individual needs of diverse learners.

One of the first steps in building a effective partnership with educators is open and consistent communication. This means actively participating in meetings, conferences, and discussions about your child's progress and educational plan. Share your observations, ask questions, and express any concerns you might have. The goal is to understand your child's strengths and challenges thoroughly, enabling educators to tailor their teaching methods to your child's unique learning style.

Educators bring a wealth of knowledge and experience to the table, and their insights can be invaluable in creating a supportive learning environment. Trust their professional judgment but also be prepared to advocate for your child's needs if necessary. Sometimes, adjustments or accommodations might be required to ensure your child has the best possible chance to succeed. Being an active, engaged participant in your child's education can help you identify when these changes are needed and work with educators to implement them effectively.

In addition to regular communication, establishing clear goals and expectations is crucial. Collaborative goal-setting can provide a roadmap for your child's educational journey, outlining specific targets for academic, social, and emotional development. These goals should be realistic and achievable, reflecting your child's unique abilities and potential. Regularly reviewing and adjusting these goals keeps everyone aligned and focused on the child's best interests.

Mutual respect and understanding form the backbone of any successful partnership. Recognize the challenges educators face in balancing the needs of multiple students while providing individualized support. Similarly, expect educators to appreciate the unique perspective you bring as a parent who intimately knows your child. Respectful, constructive dialogue fosters a collaborative atmosphere where both parties feel valued and heard.

It's also essential to understand and navigate the legal aspects of special education. Familiarize yourself with the Individualized Education Plan (IEP) process, your child's rights under the Individuals with Disabilities Education Act (IDEA), and any applicable state regulations. Knowledge of these frameworks empowers you to advocate effectively for your child's needs and ensures that educators comply with all legal requirements.

Enrichment activities and extracurricular programs can significantly enhance your child's educational experience. Work with educators to identify opportunities that align with your child's interests and capabilities. Whether it's a specialized tutoring program, a social skills group, or an extracurricular club, these activities can provide additional support and foster a sense of community and belonging for your child.

Professional development for educators is another critical aspect of building effective partnerships. Encourage and support ongoing training and education for teachers and staff to stay updated on the latest research and best practices in special education. This commitment to continuous improvement can directly benefit your child by ensuring they have access to the most effective educational strategies and interventions.

Your involvement doesn't end at the classroom door. Stay engaged in school events, volunteer opportunities, and parent-teacher organizations. Building a presence in the school community reinforces the importance of education in your child's life and helps you stay connected with educators and other parents who can offer support and advice.

Remember that building partnerships with educators is an ongoing process requiring time, effort, and patience. Be prepared for occasional setbacks or misunderstandings and approach them as opportunities for growth and improved collaboration. Flexibility and resilience are key qualities that will serve both you and your child well throughout their educational journey.

Lastly, never underestimate the power of positive reinforcement. Acknowledging and celebrating the efforts and achievements of both your child and their educators can go a long way in maintaining a supportive and motivated team. Recognition of progress, no matter how small, boosts morale and encourages continued dedication and hard work.

"Alone, we can do so little; together, we can do so much." - Helen Keller's words underscore the immense potential that comes from working together. By fostering strong, collaborative relationships with educators, you are playing a pivotal role in your child's success. Through shared commitment, mutual respect, and continuous communication, you can create an educational environment where your child is not just accommodated but celebrated for their unique strengths and abilities.

Navigating Special Education continually evolves, and your partnerships with educators will be a critical component of that journey. In the next sections, we will delve deeper into recognizing developmental differences and provide strategies for effectively advocating for your child's needs. Remember, every step you take in building these partnerships brings you closer to unlocking your child's full potential. So, take each opportunity to engage, learn, and collaborate, always keeping your child's best interests at the heart of every decision.

Chapter 8:
Health and Nutrition:
Fueling Development

Health and nutrition are the cornerstones of your child's growth journey, influencing not just their physical development but also their cognitive and emotional well-being. Establishing healthy eating habits early on sets the stage for a lifetime of good health, enabling children to build the necessary energy and resilience to explore and engage with the world around them. Understanding their nutritional needs at each developmental stage can be transformative, empowering you to make informed choices that support their unique growth trajectory. By fostering a balanced diet rich in essential vitamins and minerals, you're providing the fuel they need to thrive, from the rapid growth spurts of infancy to the complex developmental milestones of their tween years. Remember, nourishing their body is just as crucial as nurturing their mind and spirit, setting the foundation for a lifetime of healthy living and robust development.

Establishing Healthy Eating Habits

Our children's nutrition forms the cornerstone of their physical and cognitive growth. As we navigate their journey towards adulthood, establishing healthy eating habits is not just beneficial—it's essential. Early dietary patterns often set the stage for lifelong habits, making the formative years a prime opportunity to instill a love for nutritious foods.

Growing Together

In today's fast-paced world, busy schedules, and the allure of convenience foods can make healthy eating seem like a daunting challenge. But remember, it's entirely attainable with a bit of planning and insight. Let's break it down and explore practical strategies to develop a balanced and nourishing diet for your child.

Start by creating a positive environment around food. It isn't just the type of food that matters, but also the context in which it's eaten. Family meals, for instance, are a golden opportunity for modeling healthy eating habits. Children who eat with their families tend to consume more fruits, vegetables, and whole grains, and are less likely to develop eating disorders. Make meal times about connection and positivity, not just nutrition.

It's vital to involve children in the process. Allow them to assist in meal planning and preparation. Not only does this give them a sense of ownership, but it also piques their curiosity about new foods. Start with age-appropriate tasks like washing vegetables, stirring ingredients, or setting the table. As they grow older, allow them to take on more responsibility. Studies show that children who are involved in food preparation are more likely to try and enjoy new dishes.

Another crucial step is to introduce a wide variety of foods early on. The more flavors and textures they experience in their formative years, the more adventurous their palate will become. Don't be disheartened by initial rejection. It can take multiple exposures—sometimes up to ten or fifteen times—before a child begins to accept a new food. Patience and persistence are key.

Balance is the bedrock of healthy eating. Aim to include all food groups in your child's diet: fruits, vegetables, whole grains, lean proteins, and dairy. Each group offers essential nutrients that contribute to overall health and growth. For example, vegetables and fruits are packed with vitamins and antioxidants, whole grains provide long-lasting energy, lean proteins support muscle growth, and dairy products are vital for bone health.

Portion control is another aspect that often goes unnoticed but is equally important. Teaching children about portion sizes helps them understand how much food they need to feel satisfied without overeating. Use smaller plates and bowls designed for children to help manage portions appropriately. Remember, a child's dietary needs will vary as they grow, so adjust portions accordingly.

Let's talk about beverages. Water should be the primary drink for hydration. It's calorie-free and essential for almost every bodily function. Encourage your kids to drink water throughout the day. Limit sugary drinks like soda and juice, which can lead to unnecessary calorie intake and dental problems. If your child needs a bit of flavor, try infusing water with slices of fruit.

When it comes to snacks, think of them as mini-meals that offer an opportunity to add nutrition to your child's day. Opt for nutrient-dense options such as fruit, yogurt, nuts, or whole-grain crackers. Avoid snacks high in sugar and unhealthy fats. Keeping healthy snacks readily available can help children make better choices when hunger strikes.

Don't forget about the importance of breakfast. It's often called the most important meal of the day for a reason. A nutritious breakfast provides energy, improves concentration, and sets the tone for healthy eating throughout the day. Aim for a balance of protein, fiber, and healthy fats. Think oatmeal with fruit and nuts, whole-grain toast with avocado, or yogurt with granola and berries.

Food should never be used as a reward or punishment. This practice can create unhealthy relationships with eating and food. Instead, encourage positive behaviors in other ways that do not link emotions to food consumption.

Be mindful of external influences. As kids grow, their exposure to dietary advice from peers, media, and advertisements increases. Teach them critical thinking skills to evaluate the information they encounter. Help them understand the long-term benefits of healthy eating versus the instant gratification of junk food.

Furthermore, identify and address any potential food sensitivities or allergies early on. This can prevent discomfort and health issues down the line and ensure your child's diet remains balanced and nutritious. Consult with healthcare professionals if you suspect any issues.

Lastly, lead by example. Children are keen observers and often mimic the behaviors of their parents. Make a habit of eating nutritious foods yourself. Show them that you prioritize your health and they're likely to follow suit.

If all this seems overwhelming, take it step by step. Small, consistent changes can lead to significant long-term benefits. Remember, establishing healthy eating habits is a journey, not a sprint. Through patience, encouragement, and consistency, you'll help your child develop a positive relationship with food that fuels their development and supports their overall well-being.

The journey to instilling these habits might have its ups and downs, but the effort is worth the reward. Just imagine your child growing up with a body and mind well-nourished for success—what greater gift could there be?

Understanding Nutritional Needs at Each Development Stage

The journey of parenthood is a beautiful mosaic of nurturing and guiding your child through numerous stages of growth and development. A crucial aspect of this journey is understanding and meeting your child's nutritional needs at each developmental stage. Children are not just small adults; their dietary requirements vary considerably as they grow. Ensuring they receive the right nutrition is akin to fueling a high-performance engine, one that adapts and evolves over time.

During the first year, nutrition is straightforward yet profoundly important. Breast milk or infant formula provides almost all the nutrients an infant needs. It's a time when the baby's digestive system is still developing. Frequent feedings are crucial as infants have small stomachs, requiring nourishment almost every two to three hours. At around six months, introducing solid foods becomes essential. Start with iron-fortified cereals, pureed vegetables, and fruits to complement breast milk or formula. This transition phase not only supports their rapid physical growth but also aids in developing taste preferences and feeding skills.

The toddler years, from one to three years of age, bring a whirlwind of activity and enormous growth spurts. Their nutritional needs expand too. Toddlers need a balanced diet rich in protein, fats, carbohydrates, vitamins, and minerals. This stage is notorious for picky eating as toddlers exert their newfound independence. Offering a variety of foods can encourage diverse tastes. Calcium and vitamin D take center stage to support burgeoning bone growth. Healthy snacks play a significant role during this time, serving as mini-meals that keep energy levels stable throughout their active days.

Preschool years, from three to five years, are filled with boundless curiosity and significant developmental milestones. This period is critical for reinforcing healthy eating habits. Children during this time start to mimic adult eating patterns, making family meals an invaluable practice. Balanced meals that include fruits, vegetables, whole grains, and lean proteins set the foundation for lifelong healthy choices. Iron, zinc, and fiber become important as kids continue to grow rapidly.

Implementing fun and interactive ways to involve children in meal planning and preparation can make them more enthusiastic about what they eat.

Entering the school years, from six to eight years, children's activities diversify, and with them, so do their nutritional needs. They require balanced meals to fuel cognitive functions and physical activities. Breakfast emerges as a non-negotiable meal, setting the stage for the day's learning. Complex carbohydrates, proteins, and healthy fats are essential. It's also a time to counter the allure of junk food temptations that comes with increased peer interactions. Teaching kids about the benefits of nutritional choices empowers them to make healthier choices independently.

The transitional tween years, from nine to twelve years, are marked by pre-puberty changes that demand a tailored nutritional approach. Tweens need more calories compared to younger children due to their rapid growth and increased physical activity. Nutrients such as calcium, iron, and vitamins A, C, and E become pivotal. Ensuring they consume well-balanced meals helps them manage school pressures, social dynamics, and physical transformations. Encouraging involvement in cooking and emphasizing whole foods over processed ones can foster a more rounded understanding of healthy eating.

Understanding nutritional needs is not just about what to eat but also about recognizing how eating habits evolve. Emotional experiences with food, family eating rituals, and the introduction of societal food norms all play crucial roles. As parents, it's vital to create a positive food environment. This includes promoting a balanced diet, moderation, and the idea that all foods can be part of a healthy diet when consumed in appropriate portions. Listening to your child's hunger and fullness cues can also develop their ability to self-regulate their eating.

Finally, recognizing that each child is unique and may have individual nutritional needs is key. Consulting healthcare providers for personalized dietary advice ensures that you meet your child's specific growth requirements. Integration of physical activity with nutrition further supplements their development, helping them to grow into strong, healthy, and confident individuals.

The essence of understanding nutritional needs at each developmental stage is to empower you as parents to nurture and fuel your child's remarkable journey of growth, ensuring they achieve their fullest potential, both physically and psychologically.

Chapter 9: Technology and Development: Navigating the Digital Age

In today's world, technology is an unavoidable presence in our daily lives, and this holds true for our children as well. Understanding how to navigate the digital age while supporting your child's development is crucial for their holistic growth. Technology can be a powerful tool for education and entertainment, but balancing screen time with other activities is essential. Kids need physical play, social interactions, and hands-on learning experiences to thrive. When used thoughtfully, technology can enhance learning and creativity, but it's important to set boundaries and cultivate healthy habits early on. Encourage your children to explore the world around them both online and offline, fostering a balanced development that leverages the best of both worlds. Aim to be mindful and proactive, creating an environment where technology serves as a complement rather than a substitute for real-life experiences.

Screen Time and Your Child's Development

The world today is vastly different from what it was just a generation ago. Technology is ingrained in almost every aspect of daily life. From smartphones to tablets, our world is digitally interconnected in ways that were once unimaginable. For parents, navigating this digital age presents unique challenges, especially when considering the implications of screen time on their child's development.

We all know that moderation is key, but what exactly does that mean when it comes to screen time? Understanding the impacts, both positive and negative, is crucial. Technology is a double-edged sword; it can be an incredibly powerful educational tool, but it can also have detrimental effects if not managed properly.

First, let's acknowledge the undeniable benefits. Educational apps and programs can support early learning, enhance cognitive skills, and even help children develop problem-solving abilities. Interactive games and learning apps can make education fun, engaging, and more accessible than traditional methods alone. Children can learn new languages, develop creativity through drawing and music apps, and even enhance their mathematical abilities with digital tools designed for young minds.

But remember, even too much of a good thing can be harmful. Excessive screen time is linked to a range of issues, from impaired social interactions to reduced physical activity. One of the fundamental impacts of too much screen time is the risk to physical health. Children spending hours in front of screens may experience eye strain, headaches, and problems with posture. More alarmingly, such sedentary behavior significantly increases the risk of obesity.

Let's talk about the psychological effects. Excessive screen time can contribute to anxiety, attention issues, and difficulties in school. Kids who spend too much time in front of screens might have trouble focusing on tasks that do not provide the instant gratification that digital media often does. This can make traditional classroom learning more challenging and result in decreased academic performance.

Social interaction is another critical area affected by prolonged screen time. Real-life social skills are developed through face-to-face interactions. When children spend too much time on gadgets, they miss out on valuable opportunities to practice empathy, pick up on verbal and non-verbal cues, and engage in meaningful conversations with their peers and families. This can lead to social isolation and difficulties in forming healthy relationships.

It's essential to set boundaries regarding screen time. Establish clear rules about when and where devices can be used. For example, making bedrooms screen-free zones encourages better sleep hygiene. Studies show that the blue light emitted by screens can disrupt sleep cycles, leading to less restful and restorative sleep. This, in turn, can impact a child's mood, energy levels, and overall well-being.

Creating a balanced schedule that includes ample time for physical activities, hobbies, and family interactions is pivotal. Encourage your child to partake in outdoor play, which is not only essential for physical health but also fosters creativity and social skills. When it comes to indoor activities, consider tech-free time with board games, puzzles, or simple creative play.

Now, what about family screen time policies? Watching TV or movies together as a family can be a shared bonding experience, but it's important to engage in conversations about what you've watched. Discussing the content helps children develop critical thinking skills and understand different perspectives. It's not just about limiting screen time but making the time spent in front of screens meaningful and educational.

Parents themselves are role models, and their screen usage sends strong signals to their children. If kids observe their parents constantly glued to their phones or tablets, they may view that behavior as acceptable. Demonstrating balanced and healthy screen habits is one of the best ways to teach children the same.

Incorporating educational content in your child's screen time is beneficial, but even educational content should be consumed in moderation. Pay attention to age-appropriate programming and apps that support developmental milestones without overwhelming your child. Interactive and creative apps that encourage active participation are more favorable than passive content, such as watching videos non-stop.

It's not just about "how much" screen time but also "what kind" of screen time. Quality matters. Opt for apps and games that are designed by experts in child development and education. Avoid content that includes violence, aggressive behavior, or hyper-stimulating imagery, as these can be detrimental to a child's mental health and behavior.

Parents can also integrate technology into family routines in creative and balanced ways. For example, use cooking apps to find recipes and involve your child in meal preparation. Or use fitness apps that encourage the whole family to be active together. These strategies can turn technology into a bonding tool rather than a point of contention.

In conclusion, the goal is to harness the positive aspects of technology while mitigating its potential harms. By setting clear boundaries, being mindful of the content consumed, and balancing screen time with other critical activities, parents can navigate the digital age effectively. It's a challenging task, no doubt, but with thoughtful strategies, we can ensure that technology supports rather than hinders a child's development.

The nuanced understanding of screen time and its impacts prepares you as a parent to make informed decisions. Remember, the objective isn't to eliminate screen time but to create a balanced, enriching, and healthy environment for your child's growth. You have the power to guide your child through this digital landscape, fostering their development in every dimension while ensuring they enjoy the best of what technology has to offer.

Educating Through Technology: Pros and Cons

As parents navigate the myriad of educational options available for their children, technology's role has become increasingly significant. On one hand, digital tools provide interactive and engaging ways to enhance learning, offering access to resources that can cater to various learning styles and needs. Apps and educational games can make subjects like math and reading more appealing, turning screen time into productive learning opportunities. On the flip side, too much reliance on technology can lead to issues such as reduced attention spans, difficulties in face-to-face social interactions, and an overexposure to screens that might impact physical health. Therefore, it's crucial to find a balanced approach where technology complements traditional learning methods without overshadowing essential human elements like empathy, creativity, and critical thinking. Setting clear boundaries on screen time and encouraging varied educational activities can help in harnessing the positive aspects of technology, while mitigating its potential drawbacks.

Setting Boundaries and Encouraging Balance in today's digital age isn't just about limiting screen time; it's about guiding your child's relationship with technology to foster a balanced, healthy lifestyle. This requires a thoughtful approach that intertwines educating through technology while knowing when, and how, to set boundaries. When done right, it empowers children to leverage digital tools for learning without letting them overwhelm their developmental process.

Let's address the elephant in the room: technology is pervasive. For many parents, it feels like an uninvited guest that's decided to stay indefinitely. But digital tools can be incredible allies in our quest to educate our children. From interactive learning apps to virtual classrooms, technology offers unprecedented opportunities to enrich a child's educational journey. However, these benefits come hand-in-hand with potential pitfalls, making it crucial for parents to strike a balance.

Encouraging a healthy tech balance starts with setting boundaries. This involves defining clear rules about when and how technology should be used. It's not just about draconian limits, but about creating a family tech plan. This plan could include specific times when screens are allowed, such as for educational purposes or during designated free time. By establishing these guidelines, you help your child develop a disciplined approach to technology, making it a tool rather than a distraction.

One of the most effective strategies for setting boundaries involves leading by example. Children are keen observers and often mimic the behavior they see. If they witness you constantly glued to your devices, it's likely they'll follow suit. Design tech-free zones or times at home, such as during meals or family gatherings. By demonstrating that screens aren't the focal point of life, you instill the value of presence and engagement in other activities.

A vital part of encouraging balance is helping your child recognize the distinction between different types of screen usage. Not all screen time is created equal. Watching videos or playing games is markedly different from interactive learning or video chatting with family. Educate your children about these differences and why some activities are worth more screen time than others. This way, they can make informed decisions about their screen usage as they grow older.

Involve your child in the process of creating these boundaries. When children understand the reasoning behind rules, they're more likely to respect them. Sit down as a family and discuss the importance of balanced tech usage. Outline the potential negative effects of excessive screen time, such as its impact on sleep, physical activity, and social interactions. When kids feel that they have a say in setting these boundaries, there's a greater chance they'll adhere to them.

Technology shouldn't replace traditional forms of learning and interaction but complement them. Encourage your child to engage in diverse activities beyond the digital screen. Whether it's reading books, playing outdoor games, or engaging in creative hobbies like painting or building, these activities contribute to a well-rounded development. Promote a routine that includes a mix of activities to provide a balanced blend of mental, physical, and emotional stimuli.

Consistency is key in enforcing these boundaries. While it's tempting to relax the rules once in a while, especially during hectic days, maintaining consistency helps reinforce the importance of these boundaries. Flexibility is understandable, but make sure the exceptions don't become the norm. Establishing a routine that balances digital and non-digital activities can help solidify these habits in your child's daily life.

An often-overlooked aspect of setting tech boundaries is the importance of disconnecting before bedtime. Numerous studies have shown that screens can interfere with sleep due to the blue light emitted, which affects melatonin production. Encourage a digital curfew, such as no screens an hour before bedtime. This can significantly improve sleep quality and overall well-being, allowing your child to rest and recharge fully.

Focus on Quality over Quantity. Rather than merely reducing screen time, emphasize the need for engaging with high-quality, educational content. Guides and reviews of educational apps, shows, and websites can help you select beneficial digital content. Consider platforms that provide educational games, puzzles, and interactive lessons that align with your child's interests and developmental stage.

Being tech-savvy yourself can be a game-changer. The more you know about the tools and platforms your child is using, the better equipped you'll be to guide them. Familiarize yourself with the settings and parental controls available on these devices. These features can help you monitor and regulate usage, ensuring your child accesses appropriate content and adheres to the established boundaries.

Of course, it's not all about policing and monitoring. Open the lines of communication with your child. Talk about their experiences and feelings regarding technology. Ask open-ended questions about what they enjoy and what bothers them. This dialogue can provide insights into how they're using technology and help you identify any potential issues early on. It also builds trust, showing your child that you're interested in their digital life and wellbeing.

Never underestimate the power of positive reinforcement. Rewarding your child for complying with tech boundaries can motivate them to stick with the plan. This could be as simple as verbal praise or as rewarding as a family outing or an extra story before bed. Positive reinforcements can make the process of setting limits more enjoyable for everyone involved.

Physical & mental health are intertwined with balanced tech usage. Encourage regular physical activities and ensure they get ample time outdoors. Nature walks, sports, or even playing in the backyard can serve as excellent counterbalances to screen-based activities. Physical activity not only benefits their health but also promotes better concentration and mood regulation, essential for learning and development.

Promote social interactions beyond digital screens. Encourage playdates, group activities, and family interactions that don't involve technology. Social skills are honed through face-to-face interactions, and these experiences are irreplaceable by any digital means. Children learn empathy, cooperation, and communication skills through direct contact, essential for their emotional development.

Ultimately, guide your child into becoming a responsible digital citizen. Teach them the principles of digital etiquette, online safety, and the implications of their digital footprint. Educating your child about these aspects prepares them to navigate the digital world responsibly, understanding both its potentials and risks.

Finding this balance isn't a one-size-fits-all process. What works for one family might not work for another. It's about trial, error, and constant adjustment. Keep an open mind and be willing to adapt as your child grows and their needs change. By setting boundaries and encouraging balance, you're equipping your child with the skills they need to thrive in a technology-rich world, while ensuring their overall development remains on a healthy trajectory.

Remember, you're not alone in this journey. Resources and communities exist to support you, offering advice, shared experiences, and up-to-date information about navigating digital parenting. Leverage these resources to stay informed and supported as you help your child develop a balanced, healthy relationship with technology.

Chapter 10: Emotional Resilience: Building Coping Skills

In the complex journey of raising a child, emotional resilience emerges as a cornerstone for navigating life's adversities. Teaching children how to identify and express their feelings is crucial, as it lays the foundation for effective coping mechanisms and mental durability. Practical, empathetic approaches to managing stress and anxiety can empower young minds, turning potential obstacles into growth opportunities. By fostering a supportive environment and encouraging open dialogue, parents can help their children develop robust skillsets to face challenges head-on and maintain a positive outlook. This chapter delves into actionable strategies that parents can integrate into daily life, ensuring their children not only survive but thrive amidst the inevitable ups and downs of growing up.

Identifying and Expressing Emotions

Identifying and expressing emotions are fundamental skills that lay the groundwork for a child's emotional intelligence and resilience. From the first wail of a newborn to the complex emotions of a pre-teen, understanding how children recognize and communicate their feelings is crucial for their overall development.

In the earliest months, babies don't have the words to express what they feel. Instead, they rely on cries, coos, and facial expressions. This period is your first opportunity to tune into your child's emotional world. Observing and responding to these cues fosters a sense of security and attachment, which are critical for healthy development. When a baby cries, they're not just seeking comfort; they're communicating. Recognizing the varied cries - hunger, discomfort, fatigue - allows parents to meet their child's needs promptly, reinforcing the infant's trust and emotional connection.

As children grow into toddlers, their emotions become more varied and complex. Toddlers can experience a wide array of emotions but often struggle to express them verbally. Tantrums, meltdowns, and seemingly irrational fears or frustrations are all part of this phase. It's essential to remain patient and understand that these behaviors are often a response to their limited ability to articulate feelings. Teaching toddlers simple emotion words like "happy," "sad," "angry," or "scared" can be incredibly empowering. When children have a vocabulary to label their emotions, they're less likely to become overwhelmed by them.

During the preschool years, children start to develop a more nuanced understanding of emotions in themselves and others. This age is ripe for introducing concepts of empathy and emotional regulation. For instance, books and stories that involve characters experiencing a range of emotions can be particularly effective. Ask open-ended questions like, "How do you think he feels?" or, "What would you do if you were her?" This encourages children to think about emotions in context, promoting both self-awareness and empathy.

Role-playing is another effective tool for helping children identify and express emotions. Through play, children experiment with different emotional responses in a safe and controlled environment. Pretending to be happy, sad, or angry can demystify these feelings and give children a broader emotional repertoire. Encouraging children to play out scenarios with dolls or action figures can also provide insight into their emotional state and help them practice handling various emotions.

Another aspect of teaching emotional expression is modeling behavior. Children are astute observers and often mimic the emotional responses of the adults in their lives. Demonstrating healthy ways to express emotions - like calmly discussing a problem rather than shouting or withdrawing - provides a powerful example for your child. It's not about being perfect; it's about showing that it's okay to feel a range of emotions and to express them constructively.

It's also important to create an environment where emotions are welcomed, not shunned. Let your child know that all emotions are valid and that it's okay to feel sad, angry, or scared. How you react when your child expresses their emotions can either affirm or negate their feelings. For example, dismissing a child's worries as trivial can make them feel misunderstood and less likely to express their emotions in the future. Instead, validate their feelings by acknowledging them and providing comfort or solutions.

School-aged children face new emotional challenges as they engage more with peers and navigate their academic environment. Peer interactions often bring about complex social emotions like jealousy, hurt, and pride. At this stage, some children might struggle to keep up with the evolving social rules. Open communication about daily experiences and feelings can offer invaluable support. Raise questions like, "What was the best part of your day?" or, "Did anything make you feel uncomfortable or upset?" This helps children process their emotions and understand that it's okay to talk about them.

Emotion coaching can be a beneficial practice during this stage. It involves recognizing your child's emotional moments as opportunities for teaching and connection. It's a process that includes listening empathetically, helping your child label their feelings, and guiding them towards solutions. For instance, if your child is upset about a conflict with a friend, help them label their feelings ("It sounds like you're really hurt by what happened") and brainstorm ways to address the issue ("What do you think you can say to your friend to make things better?").

As children near the tween years, their emotional lives become even more complex. They start to experience more abstract emotions like embarrassment, shame, and guilt. These feelings can be difficult to manage, particularly as their social worlds expand and they become more self-conscious. It's essential for parents to maintain open channels of communication and provide a non-judgmental space where feelings can be shared. Encourage tweens to keep a journal if they're comfortable with it. Writing about their feelings can be a therapeutic outlet and a way to process emotions that might feel too intense to discuss openly.

Group activities or team sports can also play a role in helping tweens manage emotions. These settings provide an opportunity to navigate social dynamics and develop emotional regulation in real-time. Whether it's dealing with the disappointment of a lost game or the joy of a group achievement, these experiences teach valuable lessons about resilience and empathy.

Overall, emotional resilience is built through practice and guidance. By actively teaching and modeling emotional identification and expression, you're equipping your child with essential tools for their lifelong emotional well-being. It's a journey, one that requires patience, openness, and consistent effort. But the rewards are well worth the effort - a child who understands and can manage their emotions is more likely to face challenges with confidence, empathy, and resilience.

To sum up, understanding and expressing emotions are foundational skills that contribute significantly to a child's ability to develop coping skills. From infancy through the tween years, each stage requires different approaches and strategies. However, the core principles of validation, modeling, and open communication remain constant. By nurturing these skills in your child, you are fostering an environment where they can develop into emotionally aware and resilient individuals.

Strategies for Managing Stress and Anxiety in Children

Stress and anxiety are no strangers to children, even from a very young age. As parents, it is crucial to recognize that helping your child manage these emotions is an integral part of their emotional resilience and overall mental health. This section will explore practical techniques and insights that can assist you in supporting your child's ability to cope with stress and anxiety effectively.

Understanding the root of stress and anxiety in children is the first step. Kids experience stress for a multitude of reasons: a change in routine, academic pressures, social dynamics, or family issues. Observing and identifying triggers can provide valuable insights. When you notice changes in your child's behavior—such as irritability, sleep disturbances, or withdrawal—it might be a sign that they're dealing with anxiety. These behaviors are often the outward manifestations of an internal struggle.

One powerful strategy for managing stress is to cultivate a supportive and open environment at home. Your child should feel safe to express their feelings without fear of being judged or dismissed. Active listening is key here. When your child shares their worries, truly listen. Engage with their concerns by acknowledging their feelings. Saying something as simple as, "I understand why you feel that way," can be incredibly validating.

Consistency in routines can also be a bedrock of stability for children. Establishing a predictable daily schedule helps minimize uncertainty, which can exacerbate stress. Regular meal times, set bedtime routines, and dedicated periods for homework and play create a structured environment where children know what to expect. While flexibility is essential, maintaining a degree of consistency can do wonders for reducing anxiety.

Teaching your child relaxation techniques can provide them with tools to manage their stress independently. Simple practices such as deep breathing exercises, mindfulness, and progressive muscle relaxation can be introduced. For example, guiding your child through deep breathing by inhaling slowly for a count of four, holding the breath for four, and then exhaling for a count of four can help calm their nervous system.

Physical activity plays a significant role in managing stress and anxiety. Encourage your child to engage in regular exercise, be it through sports, dance, or simple outdoor play. Physical activity helps release built-up tension, boosts mood through the release of endorphins, and can improve overall mental health. Family activities like hiking or biking can also double as bonding time, reinforcing your support.

Nutrition shouldn't be overlooked when managing stress and anxiety. A balanced diet rich in fruits, vegetables, whole grains, and lean proteins contributes to overall well-being. High sugar and caffeine intake can heighten anxiety levels, so it's wise to monitor and moderate the consumption of sweets and caffeinated beverages. Regular meals and healthy snacks provide the necessary fuel for both body and mind.

Sleep is another critical factor. Ensure that your child is getting adequate, restful sleep each night. Establish a calming bedtime routine that includes activities like reading or taking a warm bath. Reducing screen time before bed is vital, as the blue light emitted from devices can interfere with the body's natural sleep rhythms. A well-rested child is better equipped to handle stress and anxiety.

Social connections offer another buffer against stress. Encourage your child to develop friendships and social networks. Having close friends can provide emotional support and a sense of belonging. However, be mindful of the quality of these interactions. Helping your child navigate friendship dynamics and teaching them interpersonal skills will prepare them for healthy relationships.

Developing a toolkit of coping strategies can empower your child to tackle stress head-on. Encourage creative outlets such as drawing, writing, or playing music as forms of expression. These activities can be therapeutic and offer a constructive way for children to process their emotions. Flexibility in coping methods ensures that your child has multiple avenues to explore when one strategy doesn't suffice.

Incorporating humor and play into daily life can be a fantastic stress reliever. Laughter reduces stress hormones and triggers the release of endorphins. Engage in fun activities with your child to lighten the mood and provide a temporary respite from stress. Even simple, silly games or storytelling can work wonders in diffusing anxiety.

Communication is the cornerstone of any effective stress management strategy. Regular family meetings where everyone can share their thoughts and feelings create an open channel of communication. These check-ins not only provide a platform for expressing concerns but also reinforce family unity. Make sure to model healthy communication yourself; children often emulate the behaviors they observe in their parents.

Seeking professional help should never be stigmatized. If your child's stress and anxiety seem overwhelming or persistent, don't hesitate to reach out to a psychologist or counselor. Professional guidance can offer tailored strategies and interventions that you might not be able to provide at home. Therapy is not a sign of failure but rather a proactive step towards your child's mental health and well-being.

Lastly, educate your child about stress and anxiety. Understanding these emotions demystifies them and can make them seem less daunting. Explain that it is entirely normal to feel stressed or anxious and that everyone experiences these emotions from time to time. Knowledge empowers them to recognize their feelings and seek appropriate ways to manage them.

In conclusion, managing stress and anxiety in children requires a multi-faceted approach. Creating a supportive environment, establishing routines, teaching relaxation techniques, promoting physical activity, ensuring proper nutrition, adequate sleep, fostering social connections, and encouraging diverse coping mechanisms are all crucial components. Open communication and seeking professional help when necessary round out a comprehensive strategy. Remember, the goal is not to eliminate stress but to equip your child with the tools and resilience needed to navigate life's challenges confidently. By doing so, you're laying the foundation for a healthy, emotionally resilient adult.

Chapter 11:
The Role of Play in Development

Play isn't just a fun distraction for children; it's a critical component of their growth. From the earliest stages of life, engaging in various forms of play helps kids explore the world, develop essential motor skills, and build the foundation for cognitive, social, and emotional well-being. The beauty of play is its versatility—whether structured or unstructured, solitary or with peers, it serves as a dynamic engine for learning. Through imaginative scenarios, kids learn problem-solving skills and cooperative behaviors, setting the stage for future teamwork and empathy. As a parent, actively encouraging and participating in play can not only enhance your child's development but also strengthen your bond, creating cherished memories and fostering a love for lifelong learning.

Different Types of Play and Their Benefits

Play is not just a way to pass the time; it's an integral component in the growth and development of a child. Whether we're talking about infants, toddlers, or school-aged children, the types of play they engage in not only vary but also offer different benefits crucial to their overall development. This section will delve into various types of play, shedding light on why each is so important.

First, let's talk about *functional play*. This type of play is often seen in infants and toddlers and involves simple, repetitive activities. Pushing a toy car back and forth or stacking and knocking down blocks are examples. These actions might seem basic to adults, but they provide young children with significant growth opportunities. Functional play helps children develop their fine and gross motor skills, hand-eye coordination, and even cognitive abilities as they begin to understand cause and effect.

Then there's *constructive play*, which typically emerges as children grow older. This form of play involves creating or building something. Children might use blocks to build towers or LEGOs to construct intricate designs. The benefits of constructive play are tremendous. It fosters problem-solving skills, encourages creativity, and enhances attention spans. It also provides a sense of accomplishment as children see the tangible results of their efforts.

Moving on, *dramatic or pretend play* is a fascinating type to observe. Children take on various roles and act out scenarios. They might pretend to be superheroes, doctors, or even animals. The benefits here are multifaceted. Pretend play enhances language skills as children narrate scenarios and engage in dialogues. It fosters empathy and social skills as they assume different roles and perspectives. Importantly, it also helps children process and make sense of their world, managing fears and emotions through imaginative exploration.

Physical play is another essential type, often seen in activities like running, jumping, climbing, and playing sports. Aside from the obvious physical benefits, like improved muscle development and cardiovascular health, physical play also has psychological advantages. It can be a vital outlet for energy and stress, promote better sleep, and increase focus and attention in schoolwork. Team sports and group physical activities further augment social skills, teaching children the importance of cooperation and teamwork.

Let's not forget about *social play*, which becomes increasingly important as children grow older. This is play that involves interaction with peers. Games with rules, like board games or playground games, fall into this category. Social play teaches children essential life skills such as negotiating, taking turns, and resolving conflicts. It helps mold their burgeoning sense of fairness and justice and nurtures friendships and community ties, which are critical for emotional well-being.

Onlooker play is less interactive but still holds value. This occurs when a child watches others play but does not join in. It's more common in younger children. However, it's a crucial stage in learning. Through watching, children learn social cues, norms, and rules of different types of play. It's a way for them to gather information and build up the confidence to eventually join in.

Parallel play, often seen in toddlers, is where children play side by side but not directly with each other. They might be building separate structures with blocks or drawing individually. Although there's no direct interaction, parallel play is essential for developing social boundaries and understanding independence within social contexts. It subtly teaches children about space sharing and can be a precursor to more interactive forms of play.

Cooperative play, which generally emerges in preschool and early school years, involves children playing together with a common goal, such as building a sandcastle or putting on a play. This type of play obviously enhances social skills, but it also teaches cooperation, leadership, and how to work as part of a team. Cooperative play builds a foundation for the complex social interactions and collaborations that are a part of everyday life.

Finally, let's consider *exploratory play*. This form of play is prevalent across several age groups and involves exploring materials, environments, or concepts. Whether it's toddlers exploring the texture of playdough or older children conducting simple science experiments, exploratory play fosters curiosity and a love for learning. It encourages a hands-on approach to discovery, making theoretical concepts more tangible and understandable.

An often overlooked but profoundly important aspect of play is its role in *emotional regulation*. Many types of play allow children to express feelings they might not have the words for, whether it's the joy of stacking blocks as high as they can before they tumble down or navigating the complex social dynamics of a pretend tea party. Play can be a safe space for children to explore a range of emotions, helping them understand and manage feelings like frustration, excitement, and empathy.

As parents, it's essential to recognize the different types of play and the multifaceted benefits each type provides. Encouraging a variety of play activities can help ensure that your child develops holistically. Create opportunities for functional play by providing age-appropriate toys that engage fine and gross motor skills. Stimulate constructive play by offering building sets, art supplies, and puzzles. Encourage pretend play with costumes, props, and open-ended toys that spark imagination.

Foster physical play through regular activities that promote movement, whether it's a trip to the park, a dance class, or a family game of tag in the backyard. Facilitate social play by arranging playdates, enrolling your child in group activities, and encouraging games that involve rules and cooperation. Even onlooker and parallel play can be supported by providing safe environments where children can observe and engage at their comfort levels.

Pay attention to your child's interests and inclinations, as these can guide you in selecting suitable play activities. However, also introduce diverse play experiences to broaden their horizons. Balance guided play, where you might lead or participate, with free play, letting children take the reins and follow their imagination.

In the grand tapestry of child development, play is a vibrant thread woven through every stage. By understanding and nurturing different types of play, you're not only helping your child develop essential skills but also fostering a joyful and meaningful childhood. So, fill those playrooms with varied opportunities, and watch as your child explores, creates, and grows.

Play as a Learning Tool

Play isn't just about having fun—it's a powerful learning tool that propels your child's development in extraordinary ways. When children engage in play, they aren't merely passing time; they are exploring the world around them, experimenting with social roles, and solving problems. This invaluable process sparks curiosity and creativity, laying a solid foundation for cognitive growth. Through play, children practice language skills, develop empathy, and build resilience. They learn to collaborate and negotiate with others, which are crucial life skills. By valuing and encouraging play, you're not just allowing your child to enjoy their childhood but also equipping them with the essential tools for lifelong learning and success. Remember, every puzzle solved and every role-play enacted brings your child one step closer to unlocking their full potential.

Encouraging Imaginative and Cooperative Play is essential for nurturing a child's cognitive, social, and emotional development. Think of play as a powerful vehicle for learning, where the seeds of creativity and social skills are sown. Here, we'll dive into how parents can foster environments that encourage imaginative and cooperative play, making it a cornerstone in their child's developmental journey.

Imaginative play, often referred to as pretend or make-believe play, is where children use their imagination to create roles, scenarios, and adventures. This form of play is crucial because it allows children to explore different perspectives and scenarios in a safe environment. Through imaginative play, children can become astronauts, doctors, or even mythical creatures, providing them with a blank canvas to express their thoughts and emotions.

One of the most effective ways to encourage imaginative play is by providing open-ended toys. Unlike toys with specific functions, open-ended toys like building blocks, art supplies, and dolls can be used in a variety of ways. These toys don't dictate how they should be played with, allowing children's imagination to take the lead. For instance, a simple cardboard box can be transformed into a spaceship, a castle, or a fort—the only limit is the child's imagination.

Parents can also foster imaginative play by creating storytelling opportunities. Reading books and telling stories can ignite a child's imagination and help them develop their narrative skills. Encourage your child to create their own stories based on the books you read together. Ask open-ended questions like "What do you think happens next?" or "How would you end this story?" These questions stimulate creative thinking and allow children to develop their own imaginative scenarios.

In addition to nurturing creativity through individual play, cooperative play is equally important. Cooperative play involves children playing together, working towards a common goal, or participating in activities that require teamwork. This form of play is vital for developing social skills such as sharing, taking turns, and understanding others' perspectives.

One of the simplest ways to encourage cooperative play is through structured activities like board games and team sports. Board games, in particular, teach children the value of rules, patience, and fair play. Furthermore, team sports not only cultivate physical fitness but also the spirit of teamwork and cooperation. Children learn to work together to achieve a common objective, leading to the development of essential social skills and a sense of camaraderie.

Unstructured group play is another avenue to nurture cooperation. Arrange playdates and create play zones where kids can come together and play freely without rigid instructions. These environments give children the chance to negotiate, collaborate, and resolve conflicts on their own, fostering an atmosphere where cooperative skills naturally develop.

It's important to remember that as a parent, your role can also be as a play partner. Engage in your child's imaginative and cooperative play without dominating it. When you participate in their world of make-believe or join them in a group activity, you are not just having fun but also modeling social skills and showing them the joy of shared experiences. Let your child take the lead and gently guide the play to encourage collaboration and creativity.

Moreover, fostering an environment that values and stimulates play is not confined to toys and activities alone. The physical and emotional space of your home can greatly influence how children engage in imaginative and cooperative play. Create a dedicated play area that is safe and inviting. This space doesn't need to be elaborate; even a small corner with basic materials and room to move can become a rich environment for creative exploration and teamwork.

Positive reinforcement and encouragement go a long way in promoting these forms of play. Acknowledge your child's creativity and teamwork efforts with praise and encouragement. Recognizing their imaginative stories and collaborative endeavors not only boosts their confidence but also reinforces the value of these activities. Comments like "I love how you turned the living room into a jungle!" or "You worked so well with your friends to build that tower!" can make a significant impact.

Also, consider integrating nature into playtime. Outdoor play can provide endless opportunities for imagination and cooperation. Whether it's building a fort in the backyard, organizing a treasure hunt, or simply exploring a local park, nature serves as an expansive and dynamic setting for both imaginative and cooperative play. Fresh air, physical activity, and the sensory experiences of the outdoors contribute richly to a child's development.

The role of play in development is profound, and when parents make a conscious effort to encourage imaginative and cooperative play, they are setting the stage for comprehensive growth. These activities are not just fun; they are instrumental in helping children weave complex thinking patterns, build robust social networks, and develop emotional intelligence. As parents, by nurturing both imaginative and cooperative play, you're doing more than entertaining your children—you're empowering them to become well-rounded, creative, and socially adept individuals.

Chapter 12: Communicating with Your Child: A Two-Way Street

Communication with your child isn't just about speaking to them; it's about truly listening and fostering an environment where they feel heard and understood. Imagine the power of actively listening and engaging in meaningful conversations that build trust and openness. It's a dynamic exchange that shapes their emotional and psychological development. When children know their voices matter, they develop the confidence to express themselves honestly. This bidirectional flow of communication is not just a tool but a cornerstone of nurturing a relationship that stands the test of time. It fosters mutual respect and nurtures a bond that solidifies through shared experiences and transparent interactions. So, let's dive into the art of effective communication and create an unshakeable foundation for your child's growth and well-being.

Active Listening and Meaningful Conversations

In the journey of parenting, one of the most empowering tools at your disposal is communication. Not just any communication, but the kind that's truly effective: active listening and meaningful conversations. Mastering this art can significantly impact your child's developmental journey and helps in fostering a nurturing environment filled with trust and understanding.

Active listening is more than just hearing words; it's about fully engaging with what your child is saying. It means putting aside distractions, making eye contact, and responding thoughtfully. When your child comes to you, whether they're sharing a triumph or voicing a concern, they seek more than just your time—they seek your presence and attention.

Imagine your child is telling you about their day at school. Instead of nodding absentmindedly while you cook dinner, stop and turn to them. Make eye contact, and show them through your body language that you're fully engaged. This simple act of attentive listening can make a world of difference in how they feel valued and understood. Responding with phrases like "I see," "That sounds exciting," or asking follow-up questions shows that you genuinely care about what they're saying.

Active listening builds the foundation for meaningful conversations. These conversations go beyond surface-level exchanges and dive into the depths of your child's thoughts and feelings. It means exploring their ideas, emotions, hopes, and fears. It's through these deeper conversations that you unravel the layers of your child's mind, gaining insights that help you support their growth effectively.

For example, when your child expresses frustration about a difficult math problem, don't just dismiss it with a generic solution. Instead, delve deeper. Ask them what specifically is troubling them. Is it the fear of failing? Is there pressure from peers? Understanding the root cause allows you to address the issue more effectively and shows your child that their concerns are valid and taken seriously.

Furthermore, creating a safe space for open dialogue is crucial. Your child should feel that they can come to you with anything without fear of judgment or reprimand. This openness encourages them to share their innermost thoughts and feelings, fostering a strong emotional bond. When your child discusses their dreams and fears with you, they're sharing a piece of their world. Responding with empathy and encouragement can make them feel secure and supported.

Empathy plays a vital role in active listening. Placing yourself in your child's shoes helps you to understand their perspective better. Empathy involves acknowledging their feelings and showing them that it's okay to feel a certain way. Statements like "I understand how that could be frustrating," or "It sounds like that situation made you really happy," validate their emotions and encourage further discussion.

Meaningful conversations also require patience. Kids may not always articulate their feelings clearly or may take time to open up. Don't rush them. Allow them the space and time to express themselves at their own pace. Your patience will not only make them feel respected but also motivate them to open up more freely.

It's also important to remember that active listening and meaningful conversations are not limited to times of difficulty or stress. Celebrate the small joys and victories in your child's life by engaging in conversations about their interests and achievements. Whether it's a new hobby they've picked up or a story from their favorite book, showing enthusiasm in their passions reinforces a positive connection.

Meaningful conversations should be a two-way street. Share your own experiences and feelings with your child. By doing so, you're modeling open communication and showing them that everyone, even adults, has thoughts and emotions worth sharing. This mutual exchange strengthens your relationship and offers your child a sense of inclusivity and understanding.

Consistency is key in all of this. Make active listening and meaningful conversations a regular part of your daily routine. Whether it's during dinner, on a walk, or before bedtime, find those moments to connect genuinely with your child. The investment of time and attention now pays off in the long run, nurturing a resilient, emotionally intelligent individual. Your child will grow up knowing they're valued and heard, which is a cornerstone for self-esteem and confidence.

In conclusion, active listening and meaningful conversations are the bedrock of effective communication with your child. They require your full presence, empathy, patience, and consistency. By engaging deeply with your child's world, you not only support their development but also build a lasting bond of trust and understanding. The journey of parenthood is filled with opportunities for connection. Seize these moments to listen actively and engage meaningfully. Your child will thank you, not just in words, but in the person they become.

Fostering Openness and Honesty

It starts with a smile, a hug, and a question: "How was your day?" Yet those simple moments can ripple through your child's life in profound ways. Fostering openness and honesty isn't about having a sit-down heart-to-heart once a year; it's about creating an environment where your child feels safe to share their world with you every day.

When we talk about openness and honesty between parents and children, we're talking about the foundation of a relationship that will endure and thrive. The key to this foundation is communication that is not only frequent but also meaningful. It's about creating a home where emotions and thoughts flow freely, without fear of judgment or repercussion. Your child should feel that their opinions matter and that their feelings are valid, even when they're difficult to express.

One of the best ways to encourage openness is by modeling it yourself. Children learn a lot from what they see, and if they see you being open and honest, they're more likely to do the same. Share your day with them, your feelings, and your thoughts. Let them see that it's okay to talk about both good and bad experiences. Be mindful of the language you use and how you react to their disclosures. If they see you responding calmly and supportively, they'll be more inclined to open up next time.

Another crucial aspect is active listening. Active listening means giving your child your full attention when they're speaking to you. Put down the phone, turn off the TV, and make eye contact. Nod, smile, and show that you're engaged in what they are saying. Reflect back what you hear: "It sounds like you had a tough day. Do you want to talk about what happened?" This shows them that you value their thoughts and feelings and that you're genuinely interested in what they have to say.

It's also vital to create a judgment-free zone. Kids, especially as they grow older, often worry about disappointing their parents. They may hold back from sharing their true feelings or thoughts because they fear criticism or punishment. Encourage them to speak openly and assure them that they'll be heard and supported, not judged or scolded. This builds trust, which is the bedrock of honest communication.

Consistency is key. If you want your child to be open with you, they need to know that you're reliable. That means being there for them consistently, both physically and emotionally. Make time for regular conversations, and show up when you say you will. Being a dependable presence in their lives reinforces the idea that they can always turn to you, no matter what.

Open-ended questions can be a powerful tool to foster meaningful conversations. Instead of asking, "Did you have a good day at school?" which might just get a "yes" or "no" answer, try asking, "What was the best part of your day?" or "What did you learn today that surprised you?" These types of questions encourage your child to think more deeply and share more openly.

At times, fostering honesty requires a soft touch with boundaries. Children need to understand that honesty doesn't mean a free pass. Structure and rules are still important, but how you enforce them can make a huge difference. Instead of coming down hard on a child for telling the truth about a mistake, acknowledge their honesty and then discuss the consequences in a loving, constructive manner.

It can be incredibly challenging to stay composed when your child shares something that shocks or upsets you. However, your initial reaction can either encourage further openness or shut it down entirely. Take a deep breath, gather your thoughts, and respond calmly. Let your child know that you appreciate their honesty and that you're there to work through the issue together.

Laughter can also be an excellent way to foster openness. Humor breaks down barriers and makes communication more enjoyable. Share jokes, funny stories, and playful moments. It helps create a relaxed atmosphere where talking feels less pressured and more like a natural part of your daily interaction.

Remember that honesty extends to you too. It's important for your child to know that you're human, with your own set of experiences and emotions. If you've made a mistake, own up to it. Apologize when necessary. Demonstrating vulnerability can teach your child that it's okay to be imperfect and that making mistakes is a part of life.

It's vital to recognize the changing nature of honesty and openness as children grow. What works for a toddler might not work for a tween. Adapt your approach based on their developmental stage. For younger kids, storytelling and play can be methods for opening up. For older kids, consider one-on-one outings that provide a natural setting for deeper conversation, like a walk in the park or a coffee date.

Ultimately, fostering openness and honesty is a continuous journey. It's not a destination you reach and then move on from. It evolves with your child and requires constant nurturing. Be patient with the process, and remember that every small effort counts. Over time, these efforts will create a relationship built on trust, understanding, and mutual respect.

In conclusion, fostering openness and honesty within your family is not just an optional add-on; it's crucial for your child's overall development and well-being. By creating a supportive, judgment-free environment, actively listening, modeling honesty, and maintaining consistency, you pave the way for a relationship where communication can flourish. This openness not only helps your child navigate their emotions and experiences but also strengthens the bond you share, empowering them to grow into confident, well-adjusted individuals.

Online Review Request for This Book

If you've found value in understanding and navigating the complexities of communicating with your child, we'd truly appreciate you taking a moment to share your thoughts in an online review, as your insights can help other parents foster deeper connections with their own children.

The Path Forward: Empowering Your Child's Growth

As we've journeyed through the intricate map of your child's development, it's essential to remember that growth isn't a checklist of milestones but a rich, evolving tapestry. Each chapter in this book has offered you insights into understanding and supporting various stages, yet the essence of parenting lies in adapting and thriving through this never-ending journey of nurturing.

So, where do we go from here? The path forward involves not only applying what you've learned but also remaining flexible and open to the individual nuances of your child's growth. It's about fostering a home environment where curiosity is encouraged, and mistakes are seen as opportunities for learning.

One of the critical aspects of empowering your child is fostering resilience. Life will throw challenges and uncertainties their way. How they handle these obstacles often comes down to the coping skills and emotional resilience you've helped them develop. From managing stress and anxiety to expressing emotions constructively, these competencies form the core of a resilient individual. In your daily life, model resilience and create an atmosphere where emotional expression is welcomed and supported.

But empowering your child's growth isn't just about emotional resilience; it's also about nurturing their intellectual and physical development. Whether it's setting up a space for imaginative play, scheduling regular physical activities, or encouraging problem-solving during homework, your involvement and encouragement make a significant difference.

Furthermore, the importance of a balanced approach to technology can't be overstated. In our digital age, technology is an ever-present part of your child's life. While it offers numerous educational benefits, setting boundaries is essential to ensure it doesn't overshadow face-to-face interactions or physical activities. Use technology as a tool for learning and engagement, not as a substitute for your time and attention.

Remember, communication is key. Your child will flourish when they know they can openly communicate with you—whether they're sharing successes or voicing concerns. Create an environment of trust and openness. Listen actively, respond thoughtfully, and sometimes, just offer the comfort of your presence.

Your role also extends to advocating for your child's needs. If there's a developmental difference or a learning challenge, building partnerships with educators and seeking appropriate resources can make a world of difference. Stay informed, ask questions, and don't hesitate to seek interventions early on. Your proactive engagement can pave the way for a more customized and supportive educational experience for your child.

Nutrition and health remain foundational to your child's overall development. Emphasize a balanced diet rich in essential nutrients, teach them the importance of healthy eating habits, and encourage physical activities that they enjoy. Remember, you're setting the stage for habits that will last a lifetime, promoting not just growth but overall well-being.

It's also crucial to appreciate the power of play. Different kinds of play—whether imaginative, cooperative, or educational—bring immense benefits to your child's cognitive, social, and emotional development. Make time for play, and join in when you can. Your involvement shows that play is not just fun but a valuable aspect of life.

Looking ahead, recognize that your journey as a parent is also about growth. You, too, are evolving, learning, and adapting. Be kind to yourself during this process. Seek support when needed, celebrate your successes, and learn from the bumps along the way. Your well-being directly influences your ability to be present and supportive for your child.

Finally, take a moment to appreciate this remarkable journey. Your dedication, love, and effort are shaping a confident, capable, and compassionate individual. By empowering them with resilience, intellectual curiosity, balanced use of technology, and healthy habits, you're providing them with the tools they need to navigate the world.

So, let's step forward with optimism and confidence. Your child is on a unique path, and with your guidance, they will continue to grow, thrive, and surprise you in the most wonderful ways. Embrace the challenges and triumphs, and remember that each stage is a precious opportunity to engage, support, and empower.

Here's to the incredible journey ahead, filled with growth, learning, and endless possibilities. Together, you and your child have the potential to shape a future full of promise and joy. Every moment you invest in understanding and nurturing your child is a step toward a brighter and more empowered tomorrow. Go forth with love, patience, and unwavering belief in your child's potential, and watch them soar.

Appendix A:
Appendix

The journey of parenting is filled with questions, moments of uncertainty, and a constant quest for the best ways to support your child's growth. This Appendix is designed to be your handy guide, providing supplementary tools and resources to further enhance your understanding and involvement in your child's developmental milestones. Whether you're looking for a comprehensive checklist of developmental stages, seeking reliable resources, or wanting answers to frequently asked questions about your child's development, this section aims to equip you with practical and actionable insights. By offering these additional layers of information, we hope to empower you with the confidence and knowledge you need to accompany your child through each stage of their remarkable journey.

A: Developmental Milestone Checklist

Let's dive straight into the core of our developmental journey: the **Developmental Milestone Checklist**. This comprehensive guide offers parents a tangible way to track their child's progress through various stages of growth. By recognizing and understanding these milestones, you can significantly enhance your child's developmental experience. With knowledge comes the power to nurture, support, and intervene when necessary.

The checklist is a roadmap. Just as a traveler would rely on a map to navigate unfamiliar terrain, you can use this checklist to guide your understanding of your child's evolving abilities. Each milestone signifies a critical step in their development, representing shifts in physical, cognitive, emotional, and social capabilities. While the age ranges provided are typical markers, it's essential to remember that every child is unique. Some may reach these milestones earlier or later than others, and that's perfectly fine.

First up, we have the infancy period, encompassing birth to 12 months. During these earliest stages, you'll observe rapid growth and change. Within the first three months, look for signs like your baby responding to sounds, lifting their head during tummy time, and making eye contact.

Moving into the four to six months range, babies start to gain more physical control. They are likely to roll over, grasp toys, and even begin to sit with support. This period also marks the start of more meaningful social interactions, as smiles become frequent, and laughter bubbles out with ease.

From seven to nine months, cognitive and social milestones become more pronounced. Babies begin to understand object permanence—the understanding that objects continue to exist even when they can't be seen. You'll witness a fascinating array of actions that include clapping hands, waving goodbye, and even some basic forms of communication like babbling or pointing to objects they want.

As your baby approaches their first birthday, expect to see milestones in communication and emotional growth. They'll likely start saying simple words like "mama" or "dada," and show strong preferences for certain people and toys. Emotional bonds strengthen, and you'll notice signs of attachment, such as seeking comfort from you when distressed.

Transitioning into the toddler years (one to two years), the checklist highlights major physical milestones like walking, running, and climbing. These physical achievements are exhilarating to watch, signifying newfound independence and curiosity. It's also the time when language skills start to bloom. Toddlers will progress from simple words to short sentences, expressing their needs and observations more clearly.

The social aspect of their development picks up pace as well. Your toddler will begin to engage in play with other children, albeit often alongside them rather than with them—this is known as parallel play. Empathy may start to emerge, marked by behaviors such as offering a toy to another crying child or sharing food.

Next, in the preschool years (three to five years), you should keep an eye on fine motor milestones. Kids will develop skills like drawing simple shapes, using scissors, and building structures with blocks. These activities contribute to hand-eye coordination and creativity.

The preschool phase also brings pre-academic skills. Look for milestones such as recognizing colors, numbers, and shapes. This foundational knowledge sets the stage for formal education, sparking curiosity and a love for learning.

Emotional development takes on a new depth during these years. Children start to understand their own emotions and those of others. You'll notice them labeling feelings and beginning to understand concepts like kindness, fairness, and empathy. They'll also start forming more meaningful friendships, which will nurture their social and emotional growth.

When your child enters the early school years (six to eight years), academic achievements become a focal point. Reading, writing, and arithmetic skills are essential milestones, each representing a significant step in cognitive development. Celebrate their growing ability to read independently, solve math problems, and write coherent sentences.

Friendship dynamics also evolve significantly at this stage. Your child will experience the joys and challenges of forming and maintaining friendships. These social relationships are essential for learning cooperation, negotiation, and conflict resolution—skills that will serve them throughout life.

Another key milestone for this age group is the growth of independence and responsibility. You'll see your child taking on simple household chores, completing homework with minimal supervision, and increasingly making their own decisions. Encourage these behaviors to foster self-reliance and confidence.

The tween years (nine to twelve years) bring their own set of milestones, marked by physical changes as they prepare for puberty. During this phase, don't be surprised if you notice sudden growth spurts and the beginning of more pronounced physical changes. Awareness of these changes can help you support your child through what can be a confusing and sometimes challenging time.

Cognitive complexities also become apparent in these years. Critical thinking and problem-solving skills develop, allowing tweens to tackle more advanced academic tasks and navigate social challenges more adeptly. Be sure to celebrate achievements in school projects, logical reasoning, and creative endeavors.

Social and emotional evolution takes on new dimensions during the tween years. Children start to have a clearer sense of self-concept and increasingly value peer relationships. They may grapple with peer pressure and self-identity issues, making your role as a supportive and understanding parent more crucial than ever.

In addition to tracking typical developmental milestones, it's essential to recognize that some children may follow different developmental paths. Whether due to special needs or other factors, these unique journeys are equally deserving of celebration and support. Being attuned to your child's individual pace allows you to provide the right kind of encouragement and resources.

To keep this journey comprehensive and streamlined, we've included various methods and activities to support each stage of development in other chapters. Detailed subsections provide insights and actionable tips tailored to every milestone discussed here. Use the checklist as a reference point, then delve deeper into specific areas as needed.

Remember, this developmental milestone checklist is not just a tool—it's an invitation to engage with your child meaningfully. Every step, big or small, is a moment to connect, support, and celebrate the incredible person your child is becoming. Navigate these stages with a spirit of curiosity, empathy, and unwavering support, ensuring that your child feels confident and cherished at each milestone they reach.

B: Resources for Parents

As parents, you're always on the look out for ways to support your child's development, get inspired, and find answers to your burning questions. The good news is there are myriad resources available to you that can play a vital role in your journey. From books and websites to local community programs, these resources are invaluable in helping you navigate the path of parenthood.

The first step is to build a library of essential books that cover various aspects of child development. Ones like "The Whole-Brain Child" and "How to Talk So Kids Will Listen & Listen So Kids Will Talk" can offer deep insights into your child's mental and emotional world. These reads not only provide scientific perspectives but also practical advice that's easy to incorporate into your daily lives.

Websites and online forums are another goldmine for parenting information and tips. Trusted sites like the American Academy of Pediatrics (*AAP*) regularly publish updated resources that cover every stage of child development, from infancy through adolescence. They offer articles, videos, and downloadable content that can answer many of the questions you may have about your child's milestones—both physical and psychological.

Beyond books and websites, there are local resources available to you as well. Community centers often host parenting workshops and support groups. These sessions can be an excellent way to gain knowledge, share experiences, and build a network of fellow parents. Don't underestimate the power of a local library, either. Many libraries offer story times and reading programs that foster early literacy and social skills for young children.

Schools and early education centers usually provide a plethora of resources for parents. Most educational institutions have counselors or advisors who can provide guidance on how to support your child's development at home. These professionals can also connect you with additional resources, such as specialized programs or therapeutic services if needed.

Let's not forget about the role of healthcare providers in offering valuable resources. Pediatricians, family doctors, and child psychologists can provide practical advice tailored to your child's unique developmental needs. Don't hesitate to ask your healthcare provider for recommended readings or referrals to specialists who can provide more targeted support.

For parents of diverse learners or children with special needs, there are specialized resources available. Organizations like the National Center for Learning Disabilities (*NCLD*) and Autism Speaks provide excellent tools and guides to help you understand and support your child's growth. From strategies for managing learning disabilities to finding the right educational settings, these resources can be a game-changer.

Getting involved in parent-teacher associations (PTAs) can also provide a wealth of information and support. PTAs often organize events, workshops, and meetings that tackle various parenting issues and developmental milestones. Being active in such associations can help you stay informed about your child's educational environment and find other parents who may be experiencing similar challenges.

If you're tech-savvy, consider utilizing apps designed to support parenting. Apps such as BabyCenter and Wonder Weeks offer personalized insights based on your child's developmental stage. They can provide daily tips, track milestones, and offer forums where you can interact with other parents. These digital tools can be particularly useful for busy parents who need quick, reliable information at their fingertips.

In addition, podcasts can be a convenient way to stay informed and motivated. Look for parenting podcasts that feature experts discussing everything from behavioral issues to educational strategies. Listening to these during your commute or while doing household chores can keep you engaged and learning without requiring extra time.

Don't underestimate the power of social media. Parenting groups on platforms like Facebook and Reddit can offer real-time advice and community support. While it's essential to verify the information you receive through these channels, they can provide diverse perspectives and make you feel less isolated in your parenting journey.

Lastly, consider seeking out professional development courses or certifications related to child development and parenting. Many universities and online education platforms offer courses that can deepen your understanding and equip you with specialized skills.

These programs can be especially beneficial for parents dealing with unique challenges or those interested in pursuing careers in child development or education.

In conclusion, the resources available to parents are vast and varied. Whether you prefer books, online content, community interactions, or professional guidance, there's something out there to support you at every stage of your child's development. The key is to stay curious, seek credible information, and never hesitate to ask for help when you need it. By leveraging these resources, you can feel more confident and empowered in your role as a parent, ensuring your child receives the best possible support to thrive physically and psychologically.

C: Frequently Asked Questions about Child Development

As parents, you're bound to have an array of questions about your child's development at different stages. It's an exciting journey, but also one that comes with its fair share of uncertainties. Here, we've compiled some of the most frequently asked questions to provide clarity and reassurance as you navigate this incredible adventure. Remember, every child is unique, and while general milestones exist, there is a range of normal development.

When should my baby start walking?

Most babies take their first steps between 9 and 15 months, but it's completely normal if your child starts walking a little earlier or later. Walking isn't just about physical development—it's also influenced by your child's confidence and interest in exploring their surroundings. Encouraging activities like tummy time and crawling can strengthen the muscles needed for walking. When your child does start to walk, celebrate the achievement, no matter when it happens. Each step is a milestone worth applauding!

What if my child isn't talking as much as other kids?

Language development can vary significantly from one child to another. While some children might start speaking in full sentences by age two, others might still be developing their vocabulary. By about 18 months, most children can say a few words and understand many more. If you're worried, consider whether your child is meeting other developmental milestones and interacting with you in non-verbal ways. If concerns persist, consulting a speech therapist can provide specific strategies to support language development.

How can I tell if my child has developmental delays?

It's natural to worry if your child seems to lag behind their peers in certain areas. Developmental delays can manifest in various forms—physical, cognitive, social, or emotional development. Regular check-ups with your pediatrician can help monitor your child's growth and development. If your child isn't reaching age-appropriate milestones, your doctor may recommend evaluations by specialists. Early intervention is key, and there are many resources available to support your child's unique needs.

What role does nutrition play in my child's development?

Nutrition is fundamental to your child's growth and development. A balanced diet, rich in fruits, vegetables, whole grains, proteins, and healthy fats, supports brain function, physical growth, and overall health. Establishing healthy eating habits early on can set the stage for lifelong well-being. It's also important to be mindful of portion sizes and to encourage a routine that includes regular family meals, which can teach healthy eating habits and foster strong family bonds.

How much screen time is appropriate for my child?

The American Academy of Pediatrics recommends that children aged 2 to 5 years have no more than one hour of high-quality screen time per day. For children under 18 months, screen time should be limited to video chatting. It's crucial to ensure that screen time doesn't replace activities essential for development, such as physical play, reading, and family interaction. Setting boundaries and encouraging educational content can help make screen time productive and balanced.

How can I support my child's social skills?

Social skills develop from a young age and are crucial for forming relationships, understanding social norms, and navigating the world. Encourage opportunities for your child to interact with peers through playdates, school activities, and group classes. Teaching empathy, sharing, and communication can be integrated into daily activities. Model positive social interactions, as children often learn by observing their parents.

What should I do if my child seems anxious or stressed?

Children experience stress and anxiety for various reasons, just like adults. Identifying the source of your child's stress can help you address it effectively. Establishing a routine can provide a sense of security. Encourage open conversations about feelings and teach coping strategies, such as deep breathing or engaging in relaxing activities. If anxiety seems to interfere with daily life or persists, consider consulting a child psychologist or counselor for professional support.

How important is play in my child's development?

Play is not just a fun activity but a crucial part of a child's development. Through play, children explore their world, develop motor skills, boost creativity, and learn social skills. Different types of play—imaginative, cooperative, physical, and educational—each contribute uniquely to development. Encourage a variety of play activities and participate in playtime to strengthen your bond and support your child's growth.

When is my child ready for preschool?

Readiness for preschool varies for each child, typically around ages 3 to 4. Look for signs of readiness, such as curiosity about learning, ability to follow simple instructions, basic social skills, and a level of independence. Preschool can provide a structured environment for early education and social interaction. However, it's essential to consider your child's personality and temperament when making this decision.

How can I encourage my child's emotional intelligence?

Emotional intelligence involves recognizing, understanding, and managing emotions. Encourage your child to talk about their feelings and validate their emotions. Teach problem-solving and empathy by discussing various scenarios and how others might feel. Model emotional intelligence through your actions, demonstrating healthy ways to express and handle emotions. Reading books about emotions and playing games that involve understanding feelings can also be beneficial.

What if my child has trouble making friends?

Friendship dynamics can be challenging, especially for young children still developing social skills. Encourage activities that involve group interactions, such as team sports or clubs, to provide structured opportunities for making friends. Teach your child about kindness, sharing, and listening, and help them understand that making friends takes time. If difficulties persist, talking with a teacher or a counselor may provide additional strategies and support.

How can I foster my child's independence?

Fostering independence is vital for your child's confidence and growth. Allow your child to make choices appropriate for their age, such as picking out clothes or deciding on snacks. Encourage problem-solving by allowing them to try new tasks independently before offering help.

Praise their efforts and accomplishments to build self-esteem and let them know it's okay to make mistakes as it's a part of learning.

Is it normal for my child to have tantrums?

Tantrums are a normal part of child development, especially during the toddler years when children are learning to navigate their emotions. Providing a consistent and calm response can help manage tantrums. Setting clear expectations, offering choices, and practicing patience can reduce the frequency and intensity of tantrums. If tantrums seem excessive or persist beyond early childhood, it may be helpful to consult with a pediatrician or child behavior specialist.

Addressing these frequently asked questions about child development can help you feel more equipped to support your child's growth and well-being. Always keep in mind that each child is unique, and comparing them to others should be done cautiously. Trust your instincts as a parent, seek guidance when needed, and celebrate every milestone, big or

www.ingramcontent.com/pod-product-compliance
Lightning Source LLC
Chambersburg PA
CBHW060613080526
44585CB00013B/813